ANTI-JUDAISM IN FEMINIST
RELIGIOUS WRITINGS

AAR American Academy of Religion
CULTURAL CRITICISM SERIES

Number 1
ANTI-JUDAISM IN FEMINIST
RELIGIOUS WRITINGS

by
Katharina von Kellenbach

ANTI-JUDAISM IN FEMINIST
RELIGIOUS WRITINGS

by
Katharina von Kellenbach

Scholars Press
Atlanta, Georgia

ANTI-JUDAISM IN FEMINIST RELIGIOUS WRITINGS

by
Katharina von Kellenbach

© 1994
The American Academy of Religion

Library of Congress Cataloging in Publication Data
Kellenbach, Katharina von, 1960–
    Anti-Judaism in feminist religious writings / by Katharina von
Kellenbach.
       p.   cm. — (American Academy of Religion cultural criticism
series ; no. 1)
    Includes bibliographical references and index.
    ISBN 0-7885-0043-0 (cloth). — ISBN 0-7885-0044-9 (pbk.)
    1. Judaism—Controversial literature—History and criticism.
2. Feminist theology—Controversial literature. 3. Holocaust,
Jewish (1939–1945)—Influence. I. Title. II. Series.
BM585.K35   1994
296.3'87834—dc20   94-35371
                                    CIP

Printed in the United States of America
on acid-free paper

TABLE OF CONTENTS

PREFACE

This book went through various stages of writing. It began as a dissertation in the mid eighties and was submitted to the religion department at Temple University in 1990. Since its acceptance by Scholars Press in the fall of 1993, I have integrated some of the more recent literature. The theoretical framework, however, remains essentially the same. Despite the higher visibility of the subject of anti-Judaism in feminist theology, this analysis is still timely. Those abreast of the literature on Christian and post-Christian anti-Judaism may be familiar with many of the arguments, but this book presents them in a comprehensive way and challenges the reader to recognize anti-Judaism as a coherent belief system. It sets out to prove that anti-Judaism is not a minor lapse or misunderstanding among individual scholars but that each slight distortion in the presentation of Judaism contributes to a larger religious and cultural teaching of contempt. It is not my intention to demonstrate that any one particular feminist author is more anti-Jewish than any other. Rather I want to alert the reader to the form and function of the anti-Jewish myth as it manifests itself in feminist theological writings. Feminist theology should not be singled out for anti-Judaism. Other studies have documented anti-Judaism in other theological and political movements. I hope this book will be accepted in a spirit of dialogue.

Many people have helped me along in my thinking over the years. I want to thank the faculty in the religion department at Temple University for allowing me to expand Jewish-Christian dialogue into feminist theology. In particular, I am indebted to Howard Eilberg-Schwartz, who became my advisor midway in the dissertation process, for his belief in this project and to E. Ann Matter for being on my committee. I want to thank the "Secret Society of the Sisters of the Sixth Story," Joan Martin, Ruth Zoe Ost, Barbara Hogan and

Beverly Aminah McCloud, for their gift of friendship, laughter and companionship during and after graduate school. I will always be grateful to Shulamit Magnus and Joanna Katz for reaching out and introducing me to the beauty and treasure of Judaism.

I am immensely thankful to Celia Rabinowitz of St. Mary's College of Maryland, librarian and colleague in religious studies, who spent the summer months editing my work and catching logical and grammatical mistakes. All the other members of the college community at St. Mary's College who cooperated in making this project possible are warmly commended.

Last not least, I want to thank Björn Krondorfer for being my lover, friend, soul-mate and spouse, who nurtured this work both intellectually as a colleague and practically as father to our daughter Zadekia.

INTRODUCTION

THE PERSONAL IS THE POLITICAL

As a feminist I recognize that my personal identity and biography influence this analysis in many ways. I want to acknowledge some of the experiences, assumptions and attachments in which this work is grounded.

This study is the result of my confrontation with my Other. It is the product of a German feminist, Lutheran raised and trained, who met her "first" Jew at the age of 23. Surprise over my encounter with a lively Jewish community, my personal transformation resulting from my journey from West Germany to the United States, my shift from a Protestant seminary to the religion department at Temple University in Philadelphia and my growth as a religious feminist all feed into this book. I travel in and between communities which are torn apart by mistrust, agony, fear, guilt and suspicion. The Jewish and German, Jewish and Christian, feminist theological and Jewish-Christian dialogue communities each speak in their own specific languages. In this book I try to assimilate these various languages and to create a dialogue among these communities.

While I am deeply connected to my German, Christian and feminist communities, I am also involved in a passionate struggle against antisemitic sentiments lurking behind each of these identities. My belonging in these communities is often characterized by anger, alienation, guilt, shame and frustration. As Harrison put it:

> Anger is a mode of connectedness to others and it is always a vivid form of caring. To put the point another way: anger is--and it always is--a sign of some resistance in ourselves to the moral quality of the social relations in which we are immersed. Extreme and intense anger signals a deep reaction to the action upon us or towards others to whom we are reacted (1985:14).

My generation, born after the war in Germany, was an angry generation. We were *Born Guilty* (Sichrovski 1988) into a world that had collapsed and could not be trusted. We were a suspicious generation who learned the facts about National Socialism and the Third Reich in school but were denied any meaningful conversation with those who had lived through this time. We absorbed documentaries in black and white and became accustomed to nightmarish pictures of emaciated faces and piles of corpses. A conspiracy of silence surrounded the past. Our parents and grandparents had decided that "there would be no discussion of that shameful past, no analyzing, no reflecting, no mourning and no regretting. There would be no need for answers because there would be no questions" (Reichel 1989:6). But the more "they" concealed their past behind a wall of shame and guilt, and the more "their" unwillingness and inability to take responsibility became visible, the angrier "we" became. The past created an impenetrable distance between the generations. "They" did not trust us with their experiences and memories, and "we" did not trust their declarations of ignorance and innocence.

Our anger against authority figures seemed to be a healthy emotional response to the bankruptcy of Western civilization. If one cannot be sure whether one's father, uncles, teachers, policemen, doctors, politicians or friends' parents participated in shooting, gassing, burning or starving innocent people, anger is a healthy, if incomplete and unsatisfactory, response. However, like most other of my German contemporaries I had never met a Jew. It never occurred to me that one day I would meet sons and daughters of survivors who would identify me with "them" and demand an answer from me as a German. I was completely unprepared for this encounter.

My "first" Jew introduced herself after class at Temple University. She asked where I came from and what I had been doing. I told her that I had been studying theology in Germany in order to become a minister. She responded, "Oh, that's great, I am studying theology, too. I'll be a rabbi." I was taken completely by surprise and burst out: "That's impossible!" In a flash I realized that in the residues of my mind Jews, and rabbis in particular, were old men with white beards wearing black frocks. A religiously committed Jewish woman did not match my image of what Jews were supposed to be. Why would any woman want to join "their" ranks and obsess over pointless and outdated legal restrictions? I remembered the many sermons and lectures which depicted the Sabbath as oppressive, *Kashrut* laws as hypocritical, Levites and Pharisees as chauvinists and Torah observance as blind submission under the heavy yoke of the Law. Even worse, Judaism was utterly male identified, patriarchal and sexist. I could not imagine why a politically sensitive feminist would want to identify with this religious tradition.

The realization of my inherited cultural bag of prejudices came as an embarrassment. As a critical person I had believed myself exempt from racial and religious biases. I had not been aware of any prejudgments until I met my first Jew. My views of Judaism had not revealed themselves as warped and distorted because they had never been measured by and compared to reality. This book continues the journey which began with this initial shock. It is a self-critical investigation of the various German, American, Christian and feminist communities which have contributed to my image of Judaism.

Meeting my Other was an intense experience. Nothing had prepared me for the possibility of meeting a living Jew. In my mind Jews were dead, victims of the Holocaust. What was I to say, to think or to feel? And what was I to expect from Jews? Entering synagogues for the first time was an extremely uncomfortable and distressing experience. I felt eyes followed me, detecting my Germanness and hating me. I was afraid and expected to be punished. I expected revenge and felt vulnerable and powerless. It took a very long time before I could begin to accept my guilt feelings and fears of retribution and to distinguish them from legitimate Jewish reactions to the Holocaust.

I became able to listen and to take in Jewish pain because I connected it to my own experience of hurt and anger as a woman. I tried to confront antisemitism as I would expect men to deal with sexism. Just as sexism is men's problem because it is men who rape, hate, discriminate and beat women, so antisemitism is the problem of Gentiles. Or as Sartre, quoting Richard Wright, put it, "There is no Negro problem in the United States, there is only a White problem:"

> In the same way, we must say that anti-Semitism is not a Jewish problem; it is **our** problem. Since we are not guilty and yet run the risk of being its victims--yes, we too--we must be very blind indeed not to see that it is our concern in the highest degree. It is not up to the Jews first of all to form a militant league against anti-Semitism; it is up to us (1965:152).

In the last analysis, oppression is the problem of the oppressor. Unfortunately, oppression functions in such a way that those who benefit from oppression do not feel their deformation unless the oppressed challenge the status quo. It is in the nature of privilege that it shields the oppressors from noticing the suffering which occurs as a consequence of that oppression. The suffering of the oppressed, be they poor, Black, Jewish or female is rendered somewhat invisible to those who benefit from it. Oppressors have the privilege of choosing whether to notice or to ignore suffering. It is this privilege of choice which distinguishes perpetrators from victims.

During the Third Reich a German with Jewish grandparents had no choice but to be affected by antisemitism and the Holocaust. German Christians, on the other hand, had a choice. They could either participate and support the Nazis, remain passive and watch Jews being deported or resist and get involved in the fate of Non-Aryans. German Gentiles could betray Jews, ignore Jews or hide Jews. As the children of perpetrators young Germans have inherited these choices. We can remember or forget, inquire or pretend "the past" is long gone. Young Jews and children of survivors do not have this choice. The Holocaust is an ever present shadow in their lives.

Because I am a feminist, I chose to identify with my antisemitic heritage and to commit myself to study it. However, when I began my studies I believed that antisemitism was a minor deformation which could easily be overcome given general goodwill, the right information and enlightenment. There were two events in my life which changed this naive underestimation of the force of antisemitism.

During my first Yom HaShoah observance in America in 1984 I suddenly remembered an incident I was supposed to have forgotten. When the participants at this commemoration were paired up and asked to share when they had first heard about the Holocaust, I recalled my grandfather's funeral in Germany where one of my uncles sheepishly handed me a newspaper article reporting about a Nazi trial. I was 18 years old when I read about the discontinuation of the trial against a great-uncle of mine, Alfred Ebner, who had been charged with the murder of 20,000 Jews. Ebner was present at this gathering, and later sat across from me at the same table. I had heard enough about the Third Reich in school to know that the dismissal of the charges did not mean that he was innocent. Yet the indictments against him and the ordinariness with which he participated at this funeral were so incongruous that I was unable to absorb the information. How could one person single-handedly kill 20,000 people? How could this old man, who was sitting peacefully among us, have been a killer? Who were these Jews? I had never met a Jew, and I wasn't quite sure what to make of "them." While I must have heard about the Final Solution in school, that knowledge did not help me to digest this information. My shock and anger over the newspaper report of the dismissal of the charges caused the uncle who had shown it to me to take it away. He refused to talk with me any further. When I continued pestering him he snapped angrily, "One doesn't talk about that," and left the room.

I did not forget the incident right away. Every so often I would ask my father and other relatives about Alfred Ebner's activities during the war. Invariably, my father would get angry and upset and tell me in no uncertain terms that none of this could have happened, that I should grant this old man his deserved peace, and show greater respect for the suffering he endured because of these "false" accusations. The argument always ended with my being reprimanded to drop the subject. There was no breaking through the conspiracy of silence.

By the time I participated in that first Yom HaShoah observance, I believed that this incident at the funeral must have taken place many years earlier, when I was about 13 or 14 years old. The confusion about my real age indicates how deeply I had buried the fact that one of my relatives had been an active perpetrator of the Holocaust.

After the observance, I decided to approach my family again about Alfred Ebner. In a letter to the uncle who had shown me the clipping, I asked why he had shared it with me. Secretly, I hoped that he had intended to defy the family-imposed conspiracy of silence, but he never answered my letter. Several months later my father called because my letter had been forwarded to him. He reiterated that Ebner could not have committed those crimes. He said that Ebner was accused of loading a train with people destined for a concentration camp which, he argued, was impossible because those railroad tracks had already been bombed. My father's story depicted Ebner as someone who had worked for the railroad and had unwittingly been involved in the transportation of Jews. Several months later, my sister called to let me know that my letter had created a stir in the family and that she had heard that Ebner had worked as a camp guard somewhere in Rumania. I then started to look through the indexes of various histories of the Holocaust but could not find any information to corroborate this rumor.

I am describing these dynamics in some detail because they are typical of the conspiracy of silence present in many German (Christian) families, a silence which disguises our families' participation in the victimization and murder of Jews. And despite the younger generation's overall mistrust of the older generation, concrete bits of information concerning our own family remain frightening and obscure enough to prevent further investigation.

In the fall of 1988, during the writing of my dissertation, I decided to use my academic credentials and university stationary to write to the Prosecuting Attorney in Ludwigsburg, Germany, who had prepared the indictments. It took another year to locate the files of Alfred Ebner's trials in Hesse's state archives in Wiesbaden. On October 10, 1989, I finally held the indictments against Ebner in my hand. As I began to read them my last clandestine hopes that he had been wrongly accused were crushed. My sense of victory over the conspiracy of silence faded quickly when I started to read the charges. As the "deputy district commissioner" and "specialist for Jewish affairs" in Pinsk, Soviet Union, my great-uncle was charged with "several hundred cases of malicious and cruel murder." He came to Pinsk in the fall of 1941 and set up the Ghetto where he engaged in every imaginable cruelty until, by December of 1942, the Jewish inhabitants of Pinsk were dead or in hiding. Among his crimes specified in the indictments were the shooting of two men because they carried a stick of butter into the Ghetto; the shooting of 40 sick and retarded Jews from the hospital in Pinsk; the killing of 280 Jewish women and men and 12 to 15 Jewish children from the Ghetto of Mokrow by giving orders for them to march into the woods, undress and step into their graves to be shot; the murder of 15 Jewish members of the *Judenrat* on October 10, 1942; the "wild shooting" of 400 people in the yard of the Pinsk hospital during which he screamed that all Jews had to be exterminated and that no one would be allowed to survive; and the selection and murder of 10 to 12 members of the Jewish intelligentsia from the prison of Pinsk after the Ghetto had been dissolved.

Although my request to read the 60 volumes of trial documents located in the archives in Wiesbaden was initially denied because of a 1989 law which protects the privacy of defendants and witnesses, I was able find more information in the archives of the Holocaust Memorial Museum in Washington, DC. There, I discovered Nahum Boneh's history of the Pinsker Ghetto. In this detailed account, a witness from the women's room of the prison describes Ebner:

> With a little gesture of his finger to the right or the left he decided whether a person should live or die. I remember how, on the first day, he had the dentist Mrs. Beckman and her brother's fiancee taken out of the cell and shot. . . . In those days Ebner was very active and visited the prison frequently, and every visit meant a death sentence for another number of Jews (1977:126).

For these one and a half years of administering the smooth running of the Nazi death machine in Pinsk and the specific incidents of beating and shooting individuals, Ebner was not convicted. As I am writing this I still catch myself wondering whether I truly believe that my great-uncle, who died several years ago, is really identical with this ruthless person who terrorized Pinsk. How can these two men be the same? The fact that men like my great-uncle were allowed to go without penalty belittled and denied the existence of their crimes. The immediate reintegration of these criminals into family and society reinforced antisemitism. The lack of punishment sustained the illusion that the Holocaust had nothing to do with one's own family, or worse yet, had never occurred.

In Stuttgart in 1964, 54 witnesses testified against Ebner. A second trial in Frankfurt in 1968 produced 157 witnesses. Yet he was not convicted. Like 54,000 other trials in postwar West Germany, this one ended without a conviction. In 1978, Ebner's trial was discontinued because of his heart condition. Ralph Giordano (1987) speaks of a *Zweite Schuld*, a second guilt, with respect to Germany's moral and political failure to confront and disassociate from mass murder. As angry as I am at the criminal justice system, I am even more bewildered by my family's failure to expel a mass murderer from their midst. When my parents married in 1959 they chose Alfred Ebner, the husband of my father's aunt, as their best man. When he was in prison awaiting trial my father raised funds for his bail. Throughout this time my father maintained Ebner's innocence and made special efforts to incorporate him into the family. My extended family must have believed that "all Jews lie" in order to rally around and protect a mass murderer from legal, financial and emotional harm. Unwittingly, I was nursed on antisemitism. It was woven into the very fabric of my family. As far as I know, Alfred Ebner felt justified killing human beings because they were Jewish and never regretted his deeds. Except for my mother, my family denied and continues to deny the truth of his crimes because the charges were made by Jews. The conspiracy of silence, this web of secrets, lies and deceptions, conceals the persistence of active and deadly antisemitism.

During my first year in America, whenever I was asked whether Germans are still antisemitic, I answered in the negative. I could not recall having ever heard anybody espouse the antisemitic ideology promoted by the Nazis. I realize now that there was no need for such blatant expressions because antisemitism existed as a silent consensus which had gone underground and become invisible. Of course, there were some statements of dislike of Jews in my family but I failed to relate those harmless prejudices to the brutal violence of the Holocaust. I dismissed these seemingly innocuous remarks and was horrified to acknowledge that they had, in effect, helped to shelter a mass murder. This realization added to my growing interest in Jewish-Christian dialogue which has begun to critically analyze any and all Christian statements about Judaism in light of the Holocaust. After Auschwitz even the slightest remark maintaining the inferiority of Jews must be seen as a potential justification of the Nazi murderers. The only thing I can do for the 20,000 Jews of Pinsk murdered by my great-uncle is to commit my work to eradicate the ideology which caused their deaths.

The other event which forced me to take antisemitism more seriously involved the German feminist community. When I returned to Germany in 1985 my former feminist peace group presented me with Gerda Weiler's *Ich verwerfe im Lande die Kriege* (1984) for my birthday. It had just been published and was a bestseller among feminists. After reading the first few pages of this investigation of matriarchal remnants in the Old Testament, I was appalled at the depiction of Judaism. Weiler described Judaism as a viciously sexist religion whose patriarchal message had conquered the whole world. She stereotyped Judaism as militaristic, legalistic and intolerant and alleged that Judaism "exterminated" matriarchal cultures and killed the Goddess.

I decided to write a book review which critiqued Weiler's portrayal of Judaism as antisemitic. I felt embarrassed and betrayed by this book which so powerfully and unconsciously incorporated anti-Jewish stereotypes. I was worried about the fact that my feminist friends seemed not to understand or share my concerns. But deep down I was convinced that those who read the book review would agree with my analysis that Weiler's representation of Judaism perpetuated dangerous distortions and stereotypes.

Instead, my book review, titled "Antisemitismus in biblischer Matriarchatsforschung?" (1986a), unleashed a storm of disapproval and indignation. Letters to the editor poured into the feminist periodical *Schlangenbrut* between 1987 and 1988.[1] My review and a subsequent article (1987) were called "defamatory" (16:44), "out-

---

[1] All translations from German are mine. References to articles and letters in *Schlangenbrut* include issue and page numbers.

rageous" (17:34,36), "polemical" (18:31) and "pamphlet-like" (18:29,38). My motivations were variously identified as "fanaticism" (18:31), "careerism" (18:30), *"Profilierungsgelüste"* (ego trip) (16:24) and "rivalry" (17:34). I was suspected of having a *"Judenkomplex"* (Jew complex), of being a "better Jew" (18:30), of "trashing" other women (17:34) and of intending to "silence research on matriarchy" (17:35). One critic described my motivations thus:

> Somebody who so thoughtlessly packs others into boxes with such devastating labels as anti-Semitism/anti-Judaism, pins a star with reversed meaning on their coats, intends to burn them and, I would suspect, has not really understood how terrible what has happened here a few decades ago here really was (18:31).

Had I lived in Germany at the time, I might never have touched the subject again. Neither I nor the editors of *Schlangenbrut* were prepared for this outburst. Rather than responding to specific content, most of the attacks objected to the fact that the subject had been raised at all. The resistance to the discussion of anti-Judaism demonstrated that women were emotionally invested in their distorted images of Judaism. This insight jolted the German feminist community into the realization that antisemitism had not ceased in the "hour zero" in 1945, as we had been led to believe. A group of German feminist theologians emerged who actively confronted anti-Judaism. Two anthologies were published which addressed issues of anti-Judaism in Christian feminist theology (Schaumberger 1987; Siegele-Wenschkewitz 1988). Eventually, Gerda Weiler edited her book and republished it under a different title (1989). A group of well-known German feminist theologians publicly denounced anti-Judaism (Jensen 1988). Numerous conferences, lectures and courses on this topic have been organized. These efforts helped to alert and educate religious feminists about (their own) antisemitism.

In the first chapter of my own contribution to this dialogue I will delineate the discussions of anti-Judaism in the German and American feminist communities over the course of the last ten years. These dialogues have left an impact on feminist writings, and newer books in the area of Christian and neo-pagan feminist theology are now being written in light of these conversations. However, in some instances, these changes are cosmetic and remain on the linguistic level without touching the overall theological framework. I argue in my last chapter that it is not sufficient to eliminate the teaching of contempt from feminist writings but that we must replace it with a teaching of respect. It is not enough to drive antisemitism underground, as has happened in Germany after the war. Instead, antisemitism must be permanently displaced by a conscious and consistent teaching of respect.

This imperative has great urgency as we are seemingly headed toward another upsurge of antisemitism. Antisemitism has always been a belief system able to forge alliances across class, ethnicity and culture, and it should come as no surprise that it returns with renewed force in times of alienation and political, social and economic upheaval. The media have drawn our attention to rising antisemitism in the new Russia, the African-American community and the former East Germany, each a community in severe distress. However, the focus on Jew-hatred in specific communities fails to explain why, once again, Jews become the targets of peoples' anger and discontent about their condition. One underlying reason, I submit, lies in the entrenched symbolic representation and imagery of Judaism in religious theory and practice which continue to shape (Christian and secular) social policies and behaviors. Thus, in addition to challenging the escalation of Jew-hatred in different groups, it is important to confront the theological traditions which impress the religious, moral and cultural inferiority of Jews on their followers.

WHAT IS ANTI-JUDAISM?

Most people maintain that they do not dislike or hate Jews in general, but only a specific trait or quality which is attributed to Jews. Oftentimes, an antisemitic remark is prefaced, "You know that I have nothing against the Jews, but . . .", followed by a list of interchangeable attributes: they cheat, stick together, control Wall Street or own the media. The reasons for which Jews are disliked appear fairly sensible. After all, who doesn't hate cheating, arrogance, cliquish behavior and being controlled by big business and the media? Everyday, normal anti-Judaism hides behind "good" reasons though these reasons shift in numerous ways. "If one rationale for Judeophobia is no longer relevant or sensible, another one will be found quickly" (Safran 1986:273).

The ability of anti-Judaic sentiments to alter their rationale and adopt new justifications is as powerful as it is characteristic of antisemitism. In 1879, Wilhelm Marr coined the new term "antisemitism," replacing the German term *Judenhass* which was current in the 19th century as were "Jew-hatred in English, and Judeophobia in intellectual circles, terms essentially inherited from the Christian period" (Bauer 1982:43). The old Christian antipathy seemed outdated and superstitious and, therefore, required a new, modern label. Antisemitism was to be an enlightened movement, sustained by scientific arguments from biological, anthropological, evolutionary and linguistic theory. For Katz "the spokesmen of the new movement searched for new catchwords that would express the modernity of their approach. The adoption of the name `anti-Semite,' rather than anti-Jew, was meant to suggest that it was not Jewishness, that is, the religion, of the Jews that aroused suspicion, but some aspects of their character that found expression in their behavior" (1980:4). The new term, in Katz's estimation, was merely a cover for an old movement and was changed for strategic reasons.[2] Although contempt for Jews was no longer based on religious beliefs but on racial characteristics, the Nazis defined a Non-Aryan on the basis of a person's grandparents' religious membership in the synagogue. Thus, despite the Nazis' biological and racist rhetoric, it was ultimately religious affiliation which decided the fate of millions of people. In other words, even though anti-Judaism and antisemitism are historically based on different rationales, the underlying contempt towards Jews remained the same.

The single most important difference between medieval religious anti-Judaism and modern racist antisemitism was the possibility of conversion. Until the 19th century the church held out conversion to Jews as an option to save their souls and lives. With the advent of racist antisemitism, conversion could no longer remedy the supposed racial inferiority of Jews. Conversion was the only serious conflict between the Nazis and the Christian churches during the Third Reich. Any baptized Christian who had three or four Jewish grandparents was classified as a Jew (i.e. Non-Aryan). The application of the Aryan

[2] For Mosse, on the other hand, the introduction of antisemitism marks the advent of a completely new *Weltanschauung*, racism. In his analysis racism provided a new, unprecedented ordering system which integrated traditional thought systems and transformed them: "Racism annexed every important idea and movement in the nineteenth and twentieth centuries and promised to protect each against all adversaries. Scientific accomplishment, a Puritan attitude toward life--the triumphant middle-class morality, Christian religion, the ideal of beauty as symbolic of a better and healthier world were all integral facets of racism" (Mosse 1978:xii). See also Alan Davies' critique (1979:188-208) of Ruether (1974a:183ff).

paragraph in the churches which mandated the dismissal of all ordained Non-Aryan clergy led to some resistance in the Catholic and a split in the Protestant churches because it plainly annulled the sacrament of baptism. Despite these weak efforts, the churches failed to protect their Christian Non-Aryan sisters and brothers and they hardly even attempted to prevent the persecution of the "real" Jewish community (Gerlach 1987). On November 16, 1938, the first Sunday after the *Reichskristallnacht*, the night when synagogues burned throughout Germany, when Jewish people were beaten and murdered, businesses looted, homes destroyed and 30,000 Jewish men were interned in concentration camps, only one Protestant minister was arrested because his sermon forcefully condemned antisemitism (Gerlach 1987:237). What did others preach on this Sunday of Repentance?

The Holocaust is an indictment of Christian theology as Eckardt (1967, 1974), Ruether (1974a) and Parkes (1974) have pointed out. Theological anti-Judaism is one root of racist antisemitism and, hence, also responsible for the death of six million Jews. Christianity either directly supported a "solution of the Jewish question" or, at least, prevented any organized resistance. For Parkes,

> there is no break in the line which leads from the beginning of the denigration of Judaism in the formative period of Christian history, from the exclusion of Jews from civil equality in the period of the church's first triumph in the fourth century, through the horrors of the Middle Ages, to the Death Camps of Hitler in our own day (1963:60).

As powerful and virulent as religious and theological anti-Judaism is, it is not the only root. The elimination of religious and theological stereotypes is not synonymous with the end of anti-semitism. As the experiences of various Jewish communities in their struggle against antisemitism show, each strategy against antisemitism eventually resulted in a new stereotype. Consider those Jews who became socialists because they believed that poverty, exploitation and injustice bred antisemitism. Inadvertently, they created the stereotype of the "Jewish Bolshevik." Or German Jews who believed that the Jewish religion needed "reform" in order to be accepted. Yet as religion became acceptable, Jews became unacceptable as a race. Or consider Eastern European Zionists who reformed Jewish artisans and merchants into peasants and soldiers in order to create a nation among other nations only to be confronted by anti-Zionism and worldwide opposition to Jewish statehood. Each Jewish success in combating stereotypes seems to generate new ideologies and justifications for hatred. Each strategy against anti-Judaism has triggered a new rationale for contempt. Anti-Judaism is a reality of social domination which uses different ideological justifications. Anti-Judaism can be disguised in economic, racial, political, religious and personal arguments but it always defines Jews as Other.

Throughout this book I will use the term "anti-Judaism" primarily as a theological term. But I understand anti-Judaism in the broad sense as proposed by Lloyd Gaston:

> Just as individuals can be relatively free of personal prejudice and still participate actively in a system of racism, so anti-Judaism has to do with words and their objective effects whether or not the people who speak them subjectively hate Jews. . . . If the three pillars on which Judaism stands are God, Torah and Israel, then a fundamental attack on any of the three would be anti-Jewish, i.e. the denial of Jews to exist in terms of their own self-understanding (1979:50).

This definition appeals to me because it understands anti-Judaism as a pervasive social reality in which every non-Jew participates regardless of individual intent. This book looks for the unself-conscious, small and seemingly innocent distortions of Judaism which add up and sustain more pernicious forms of prejudice. It argues that Christian feminist and Goddess theologies have added a new rationale to this list of contempt: that Judaism is uniquely sexist and responsible for the creation of patriarchy.

WHY FEMINIST THEOLOGY?

This study focuses on theological (mis)representations of Judaism in feminist theology because I am interested in and committed to feminist theology. I do not investigate feminist theology because I believe that it incorporates more anti-Judaism than androcentric theologies, including other progressive theologies. Similar studies of anti-Judaism have been undertaken for liberation theology (Klenicki 1983; Williamson 1979), process theology (Williamson 1980) and political theology (Eckardt and Eckardt 1988:102-123). This study should be understood in the context of similar projects. Anti-Judaism is not a uniquely feminist theological problem. But as a pervasive aspect of Christianity it has been adopted consciously or sub-consciously, willingly or unwillingly, by feminist theologians. Most feminists have an impeccable political record with respect to combating bigotry. Indeed, many feminist theologians have contributed substantially to Jewish-Christian understanding and dialogue while others have significantly helped and supported Jewish feminists. In many cases there is no question as to their sincere intention to avoid anti-Judaism. However, anti-Judaism sometimes exists despite good intentions and in the absence of personal prejudice.

The criterion I used to include certain representations of Judaism as anti-Jewish does not depend on an author's intention or political record, but rather on whether a particular portrayal is historically warranted, fair and balanced. A second criterion for inclusion is the repetition of similar negative descriptions by several writers. Since I am primarily interested in tracing the typical and commonly accepted beliefs which buttress the inferiority of Judaism rather than the theological thought of individual authors, I include statements by writers whose thinking about Judaism may, on the whole, be more sophisticated and careful. I feel justified in doing so because I want to show the underlying theological structures which create certain distortions as well as the accumulated impact of these distortions on Christian readers. At some points, I will deliberately accentuate some distortions in order to show potential misinterpretations and dangers.

I hope that uncovering feminist complicity in the oppression of Jews will generate dialogue and confrontation which are essential for growth. I trust that my passion and anger will contribute to bring about and give birth to change rather than disempower feminist women in our struggle for justice (see Lorde 1984:131).

Chapter I

A FEMINIST APPROACH TO ANTI-JUDAISM

THE SYMBOLIC IS THE POLITICAL

Since the 19th century feminists have maintained that religious texts and traditions support and reinforce sexual inequality and women's oppression (Gifford 1985:11-35). Sacred texts explicitly ordain women's subordination under men as God's will (1 Cor 11:2-16), portray women as property (Ex 20:17) and `helper' of men (Gen 2:18). Women are depicted as objects of male interest, scorn, concern, legislation and love, but not as subjects of their own lives. Women's will and power are discouraged and condemned as sinful. Religious texts present women as giving birth to men, marrying men, seducing men, remaining untouched by men, birthing male heirs, loving men, or outliving men. Women's roles as mother, bride, whore, virgin, wife and widow are patterned around the male who is the center and beneficiary. Furthermore, sacred texts recommend and condone violence against women as a means of enforcing women's subjection (Setel 1985:86-96; Thistlethwaite 1985:96-111). Feminists struggling for social change find that religious texts are used to justify and legitimize the social organization of the sexes as divinely ordained.

Moreover, feminists have argued that patriarchy is stabilized when God is symbolized as male, Father, Judge, King and Warrior. The masculinity of God is maintained despite protestations that "**He** is beyond gender." Feminist scholars in religion have cited anthropologist Geertz's definition of religion (Christ 1979:2,274; 1985:233; Russell 1987:43; Plaskow 1979:2) which contends that religion legitimizes social systems by establishing "powerful, pervasive, and long-lasting moods and motivations in men (sic) by formulating conceptions of a general order of existence" (Geertz 1973:90). Religion creates deep convictions in individuals about the right and righteous order of the universe and shapes the order of the world in which we live. Sexist religion justifies patriarchal reality as God's will.

> If God in "his" heaven is a father ruling "his" people, then it is in
> the "nature" of things and according to divine plan and the order
> of the universe that society be male dominated. Within this context
> a mystification of roles takes place: the husband dominating his
> wife represents God "himself." The images and values of a given
> society have been projected into the realm of dogmas and "Articles
> of Faith," and these in turn justify the social structures which have
> given rise to them and which sustain their plausibility (Daly
> 1973:13)

Since God represents authority, power, trustworthiness, strength
and justice and since God is associated with maleness, women cannot
occupy roles of power and authority. The symbolic level is mirrored
in the social reality of patriarchy which allocates power and authority
to men. Symbol systems arise out of social reality and in turn
influence that reality. The feminist critique of religion is based on the
conviction that the symbolic, religious and metaphorical spheres are
dialectically connected with political and social realities.

Feminist theology is political theology. Its theory is rooted in
the practice of women's liberation. For feminist theologians, the
struggle for women's liberation occurs in the context of religion.
Patriarchy, the socio-political and economic system of father rule,
loses credibility when theology and religious symbols no longer
support and legitimize male supremacy. Historian Lerner maintains
that

> sexism and patriarchy mutually reinforce one another. Clearly,
> sexism can exist in societies where institutionalized patriarchy has
> been abolished . . . as long as sexism as an ideology exists,
> patriarchal relations can easily be reestablished, even when legal
> changes have occurred to outlaw them (1986:240).

Changes concerning the social, economic and legal status of
women, must be reciprocated and supported by changes in the
ideological, symbolic and theological imagination. Feminist theology
promotes these changes. It critiques sexism and encourages the
creation of new theological symbols. Feminist theology fosters the
development of women's spirituality which allows women to express
their experience of the divine and to create a new language and new
symbol systems which express humanity's encounter with the sacred
more fully and inclusively. The "critical principle" which guides the
feminist critique of, and search for, truth in religion is that "whatever
denies, diminishes, or distorts the full humanity of women is . . .
appraised as not redemptive" (Ruether 1983:18). Religious texts and

traditions which support male supremacy are rejected in favor of alternatives which promote the equality and full humanity of women.

TOWARDS AN INCLUSIVE THEORY OF PATRIARCHY

Elisabeth Schüssler Fiorenza has proposed that a "feminist critical hermeneutics of suspicion" places a warning label on all biblical texts: "Caution! Could be dangerous to your health and survival" (Fiorenza 1985:130). This warning label against the potential hazards of sexism in religious texts must be expanded to include other forms of oppression. The assumption that women's health is primarily threatened by sexism has been critiqued as "false universalization of what is in fact only the experience of a particular group" (Davaney, quoted in Thistlethwaite 1989:12). It constitutes the experience of a privileged group of women: white, middle class, Christian, hetero-sexual, North American and European women. The introduction of womanist (Williams 1989, 1993; Weems 1988; Cannon 1988; Grant 1989) and other theologies generated by women of diverse ethnic, class and cultural backgrounds have led to an expanded understanding of patriarchy (Isasi-Diaz 1988; Mudflower Collective 1985; Brock 1988). Women's health and survival, so their argument goes, is often-times at greater risk because of racism, antisemitism, homophobia, class exploitation and neocolonialism than sexism. Only a small group of women experiences pure sexism. The majority of women suffers from the combined forces of sexism and classism, sexism and racism, sexism and antisemitism. Schüssler Fiorenza has concluded that patriarchy is more than gender-dualism but, rather, a pyramid of oppressions. "A woman's place" in that pyramid is not necessarily at the bottom but is determined by a number of variables:

> A critical feminist theology of liberation, therefore does not speak of male oppressors and female oppressed, of all men over all women, but rather of patriarchy as a pyramidal system and hierarchical structure of society and church in which women's oppression is specified not only in terms of race and class but also of "marital status" (1985:5).

Schüssler Fiorenza's definition indicates that women who are white, middle class, heterosexual, North American and Christian have fewer choices than the men in this group but are privileged with respect to Black or lesbian women. Compared to white Christian women, a middle class, North American, Jewish woman's choices are shaped by antisemitism. But she participates in social, racial and economic privileges unavailable to underprivileged Black Christian women. A white, poor male can assert feelings of superiority to white women, people of color and Jews but is considered socially and economically inferior to middle class white men and women.

Within this hierarchy of privilege white, middle class, Christian, heterosexual males are considered most suited for social positions of power, influence and authority, and are assumed to be best fitted to represent God on earth. Groups lower in this pyramid of hierarchies are afforded fewer choices, fewer options and less physical, emotional, spiritual and economic space to inhabit. Most people find themselves in the role both of oppressed and oppressor, privileged with respect to one group but disadvantaged with respect to another. Privilege and oppression occur simultaneously. The oppressed are not exempt from responsibility for the perpetuation of other forms of oppression. Victims of oppression are not innocent but oftentimes participate knowingly or unknowingly in the oppression of Others.

Differences among women had been subsumed under a unified "women's experience" and dissenting experiences were discounted. Lorde points out that differences create anxiety rather than joy over women's diversity.

> As members of such an [profit] economy we have *all* been pro-
> grammed to respond to the human differences between us with fear
> and loathing and to handle that difference in one of three ways:
> ignore it, and if that is not possible, copy it if we think it is
> dominant, or destroy it if we think it is subordinate (1984:115).

"In the 1980s, perhaps the dominant emphasis in women's studies scholarship has been on what is generally called `difference'" (Gordon 1986:25), specifically differences among women. Several white feminist theologians confronted their complicity in racism, antisemitism and classism and acknowledged their contribution to the silencing and overlooking of the voices of nonwhite, non-Christian women (Heyward 1985; Andolsen 1986; Thistlethwaite 1989).

Sexism, racism and antisemitism divide the world into dualistic oppositions and arrange the sexes, races or religions into pairs of superior/inferior, good/bad and dominant/subordinate. These categories do not come in neatly divided pairs. Male-female, Christian-Jewish, Black-white are artificial and reductionist categories which do not grasp the wealth of difference among people. Yet, these dualistic distortions inform our perceptions of each other and of our reality. They order our differences in such a way as to create outsiders and insiders, center and periphery. Those on the outside are marginalized and objectified. Injustice and suffering appear tolerable if they affect them, as long as they are different from us.

STRATEGIES OF MARGINALIZATION

While it is important to avoid leveling oppressions into one pattern, thus reducing sexism, racism and antisemitism into mere copies of one another, important parallels and interconnections between them have been acknowledged by a variety of scholars from different disciplines (cf. Griffin 1981:159-176; Dworkin 1983:107-147; Harding 1986:163-197; Pogrebin 1982; Ruether 1975:87-115, 1981; Gilman 1985; LeRider 1985; Fanon 1967; Trachtenberg 1983; Trevor Roper 1956:109-111). Women, Jews and people of color are assigned similar attributes, such as carnality and immanence, although in reality these groups have little in common. Simone de Beauvoir observes that these alleged similarities are the result of distorted conceptions by the dominant cultural consciousness.

> The similarities . . . are in no way due to chance for whether it is a race, a caste, a class, or a sex that is reduced to a position of inferiority, the methods of justification are the same. "The eternal feminine" corresponds to "the black soul" and to the "Jewish character" (1974:xxvii).

Oppressions do not all function the same way but the strategies which marginalize women by rendering them inferior, evil and invisible give important clues for understanding the representation of Jews and Judaism in Christian theology and culture.

The Inferior Other

Women, Jews and people of color are defined as the antithesis of the cultural norm. The defining "group is embodied with all the positive associations of the self. The Other is the antithesis of the self . . . [T]he image of the dangerous Other serves both as the focus for the projection of anxiety concerning the self and as the means by which the Other defines itself" (Gilman 1985:129-130). Women, Jews and Blacks are defined by attributes which are rejected as negative by the normative group. For instance, Judaism is defined as legalistic, materialistic and this-worldly--characteristics that are antithetical to Christian self-understanding. Similarly, the antithesis of masculinity is femininity. The natural, emotional, immanent and material drives are considered to be essentially feminine and must be subjected to male spiritual and intellectual control.

The nature of femininity and of Jewishness sometimes converge. Otto Weininger, whose *Geschlecht und Charakter* became an antisemitic and antifeminist bestseller in Vienna in 1903, concedes that "it comes as a strange surprise to those who have been thinking about both the woman and the Jew when they realize the degree to which especially Judaism is saturated by femininity" (1980:409). He proceeds to enumerate convergences of femininity and Jewishness: both lack interest in real estate (409), in Kantian rationality and spirit (411), in individuality, personality and a desire for immortality (420). Both woman and Jew exist only as a type (416) and lack morality: "In the Jew, almost like in women, good and evil are not yet differentiated" (414). Rather they are "always more lustful, hornier" (though Jewish men are sexually less potent than Aryan men [417]).[1]

Femininity and Jewishness are characterized by lack. Anti-semitism and sexism represent women and Jews as less than fully equipped human beings. Sexism contends that the male represents the norm of humanity while the female is derivative. Many prominent theologians, such as Augustine and Thomas Aquinas discussed women's lack of full humanity and doubted our endowment with a soul.[2] Definitions of what it means to be a human being are derived from male standards. Measured against these standards women are found to be lacking and appear immature, incomplete and inferior. Freud's theory of penis-envy is indicative of these androcentric assumptions (Irigaray 1985:11-112), as is Jung's psychology (Wehr

---

[1] Weininger was Jewish and committed suicide at age 23. He readily admits his Jewishness and self-hatred (1980:32-36). For him self-hatred is a virtue. Jacques LeRider places Weininger in the "category of those Jews, who are so deeply shaken by antisemitism that they internalize it and fall victim to self-hatred" (1985:210).

[2] For an anthology of primary texts see O'Faolain and Martines (1973). The Vatican's refusal to ordain women stands in the tradition of androcentric assumptions of women's defectiveness (Vatican 1977:44).

1987) and contemporary developmental theory (Gilligan 1982). Each of these theories perceives the world from a male center and declares the female deficient and jealous of male superior qualities.

In a similar vein, Christianity is taken as the normative center and Judaism is portrayed as lacking redemption, forgiveness of sins and transcendence. Jews are characterized as envious and jealous (Rom 11:11,13). In an androcentric and Christocentric culture, women are characterized by penis-envy and Jews by Christ-envy.

The femininity of Jewish men and Judaism became powerful rhetorical devices in Christian anti-Jewish polemics. The femininity of Jewish men was treated as a fact in medieval legends, alleging that Jewish men were menstruating. Originating in Spain, these legends were common knowledge in German lands by the 15th century (Ruether 1975:106).[3] In the 19th and 20th centuries, Jewish men's masculinity was denied in such myths as the "Jewish shirker" (Bitton-Jackson 1982:100) which characterized Jews as effeminate cowards who evaded military service. Moreover, as Susannah Heschel points out, both Jewish and Christian polemicists and apologists gender their polemics and cast the Other religion in a feminine light: Christian theologians depict Judaism as earthly, immanent and materialistic while Jewish apologists describe Christianity as euphoric, romantic and enthusiastic. Heschel quotes Adolf von Harnack who portrays Judaism as a clogged and dirty well (clearly suggestive of female anatomy) while Leo Baeck calls Christianity a "romantic religion," characterized by irrationality, receptivity and enthusiastic spirituality (Heschel 1988:95).

In the cultural sphere, 19th century plays and novels used the image of Jewish women to "ridicule feminist ambitions through the image of the eternal Wandering Jewess, a capricious, overbearing, willful, destructive and frustrated amazon" (Bitton-Jackson 1982:6). Feminism, together with liberalism, socialism and sexual liberation, were perceived to be products of the "Jewish spirit" and of degenerate "Jewish influences." Law and order, the purity and health of the family seemed incompatible with Jewishness or feminism. Stereotypes of femininity, Jewishness and Blackness are used to code one's opponents in order to undermine their credibility.

---

[3] The 15th century Nuremberg Meistersinger Hans Folz was well aware that "the Jews still have the *weibss Kranckheyt* [women's disease]" (Folz:1908:390). He presupposes that his audience is familiar with this legend and does not elaborate on this "fact."

In contrast to the male Jew, whose materialism and sexual depravity are emphasized, the "Jewess" has been portrayed in Christian literature as a noble and distant object of sexual and religious admiration. As Bitton-Jackson points out, "it was her [the Jewish woman's] natural prerogative to counter the negative image of the Jew whatever the image happened to be" (1982:100). As Oriental woman she is depicted as beautiful and sexually fascinating; as the veiled and protected daughter of her Jewish father, she is beyond the reach of her Christian admirers. The portrayal of her purity, courage and beauty makes her superhuman. She is depicted as a saint. Sometimes she converts to Christianity, sacrificing her love for her family, community and religion. At other times, she prefers martyrdom over conversion, and gives up her life rather than her love of faith and family.

This pedestal is the product of the combined strategies of sexism and antisemitism. The Jewish woman's saintly, sacrificial femininity serves to hide her actual oppression under both sexism and anti-semitism. Similar to the depiction of Black women as matriarchs whose energy and strength seem inexhaustible, the exaggerated femininity of Jewish women in Christian literature conceals the political reality of oppression. Sexism intersects with antisemitism in unique ways. Jewish women's femininity is emphasized as, for instance, in the stereotype of the "Jewish American Princess" and the "Jewish mother." Antisemitism and sexism collude to caricature Jewish women's femininity by magnifying their manipulative dependence on men. Racism and sexism, on the other hand, result in downplaying Black women's vulnerability and dependence on familial relationships and in objectifying them into isolated and exploitable maids, mammies and sex objects. The active interstructuring of sexism and anti-semitism, and sexism and racism, causes double distortions: the seemingly powerful portrayal of Jewish women does not lessen their actual inferiority and powerlessness but makes oppression even more intricate and invisible.

The Myth of Sin and Evil

Oppressed groups are associated with evil and feared as dangerous and destructive.[4] The Christian myth of feminine evil (Daly 1973:44-68) is symbolically developed by the figure of Eve. Christian interpretations of Genesis blame Eve, the first Woman, for the Fall of Man (1 Tim 2:11-14). Eve tempted Adam into sin and thus brought death, alienation and evil into the world. Tertullian's indictment of women is an infamous and well-known interpretation of these biblical texts:

> And do you not know that you are Eve? God's sentence hangs still over all your sex and His punishment weighs down upon you. You are the devil's gateway; you are she who first violated the forbidden tree and broke the law of God. It was you who coaxed your way around him whom the devil had not the force to attack. With what ease you shattered that image of God: man! Because of the death you merited, the Son of God had to die (De Cultu Feminarum, transl. in O'Faolain 1973:132).

Eve is blamed for the origin of evil, and with her all women are identified with it. As daughters of Eve, women are tainted by a special hereditary guilt which is atoned for and punished by pain in childbirth and subjection to their husbands. The myth of Eve creates and maintains mistrust and suspicion towards women. Even the baptized and redeemed Christian woman cannot escape Eve's curse entirely. She is treated with caution, kept out of positions of power and prevented from teaching and preaching. Women are always suspect, believed to be especially inclined towards deception, temptation and disloyalty. They are turned into a source of fear for both women and men. The Inquisitors Kramer and Sprenger, the spiritual fathers of the witch persecutions, wrote that Adam "was tempted by Eve, not by the devil, therefore she is more bitter than death" (1971: 47). The witch trials of early modernity are one of the more drastic examples of the pervasive mistrust of women as tainted by evil (Kramer & Sprenger 1971:43-47; Barstow 1994).

The myth of feminine evil and the symbolic entanglement of Eve-sexuality-death-evil-devil have severely distorted Christian

[4] For the association of Jews with the devil, see Trachtenberg 1983:57-140; Trevor-Roper 1956:109-111. For the association of Blacks with evil, see Fanon 1967:188-189.

theology. As Elizabeth Cady Stanton suspected a century ago, the dissociation of Eve from symbolic linkage with the cosmic origin of evil threatens the central Christian doctrines of the Fall and Salvation.

> Take the snake, the fruit tree and the woman from the tableau, and we have no fall, no frowning Judge, no Inferno, no everlasting punishment, hence no need of a Savior. Thus the bottom falls out of the whole Christian theology. Here is the reason why in all the Biblical research and higher criticisms, the biblical scholars never touch the position of woman (quoted in Daly 1973:69).

While women symbolize the origin of death, sin, alienation and evil, Jews take on the symbolic role of executioner of Christ. As Christkillers the Jews become carriers of sin. Jews throughout history have been symbolically identified with those who demanded Jesus' blood, and they were punished for the crime of deicide by exile, discrimination, persecution and general oppression. Tainted by evil, Jews are mistrusted and feared. During the Middle Ages, they were suspected of poisoning wells, spreading the Black Death and forming alliances with the Turks, Moors, Heretics and the Antichrist. In modern times, Jews were accused of being responsible for unemployment, communism, capitalism, high taxes, warfare, etc. A Jewish world conspiracy is believed to threaten peace, prosperity and the well-being of Gentile nations.

Jews cannot disprove this myth by "good" behavior (humble, honest, friendly, assimilated, charitable). The standard antisemitic statement, "some of my best friends are Jewish," coexists with the belief in the collective evil nature of the Jewish people. The individual "good" Jew (or woman, or Black) cannot diffuse such mythologizing which tarnishes the entire group. The exception is a constitutive part of the rule.The token Jew/woman/Black is the flip side of the mistrust directed against the whole community.

Despite the favorable (though, in fact, double-distorting) depiction of the Jewess in Christian literature, Jewish women have always been victims of anti-Jewish violence. Antisemitic assaults --often understood as self-defense against an alleged Jewish attack --have never spared Jewish women: neither the crusades, the medieval and early modern expulsions of Jewish communities, the Eastern European pogroms nor the extermination program of the Nazis distinguished among men, women or children. Oftentimes, Jewish women were doubly victimized: as mothers, they were immediately gassed with their children or became victims of sterilization campaigns; as "sexual objects" they were the targets of sexual violence in addition to other brutalities in the camps (cf. Katz and Ringelheim 1983; Ringelheim 1993:373-419; Bridenthal 1984; Rittner and Roth 1993).

Invisibility

Being described as inferior Other and blamed for evil, the oppressed are also rendered invisible. Feminists have argued that androcentrism creates a universe from which women are absent. Women are eclipsed behind their husbands' names and their labor is expropriated, devalued and banished to the background. While men's work makes history women's achievements are edited out of history.

> It is often said that women are the "backbone" of the church. On the surface this may appear to be a compliment, especially when one considers the function of the backbone in the human anatomy. . . . In any case, the telling portion of the word backbone is "back." It has become apparent to me that most of the ministers who use this term have reference to location rather than function. What they really mean is that women are in the "background" and should be kept there. They are really support workers (Grant 1970:423).

Feminists have developed several strategies to counteract women's constitutional invisibility. For instance, radical feminists propose the creation of female gynocentric space. Rather than attempting to integrate the male patriarchal Foreground from which women have been excluded, women are advised to move into the Background:

> Moronized women believe that male-written texts (biblical, literary, medical, legal, scientific) are "true." Thus manipulated, women become eager for acceptance as docile tokens mouthing male texts, employing technology for male ends, accepting male fabrications as the true texture of reality. Patriarchy has stolen our cosmos and returned it in the form of Cosmopolitan magazine and cosmetics. They have made up our cosmos, our Selves. Spinning deeper into the Background is courageous sinning against the Sins of the Fathers. . . . Moving into the Background/Center is not navel-gazing. It is be-ing in the world (Daly 1978:6).

The drive to recover the background, invent women's herstory (Collins 1979:91-137) and develop women's spirituality (Spretnak 1982) as equal counterpart to male history and theology has yielded remarkable results. Some feminists have created all-women covens and feminist spirituality groups and have (re)constructed "women's intellectual heritage" (Culpepper 1987:9). Other feminists have proposed that we seek new "heuristic models that explore women's historical participation in social-public development and their efforts to comprehend and transform social structures" (Fiorenza 1984:86). Rather than accepting women's displacement from the Foreground, the lives of women are reconstructed in the public, social and religious spheres. History is read against the sexist biases that banish women into background.

Judaism is similarly rendered invisible in Christian culture. As I will argue in the second chapter, Judaism disappears from Christian consciousness after the destruction of the Second Temple in 70 C.E. While Jews were rendered invisible socially and politically in the larger Christian world, the definition of Jewish identity has never completely fallen into the hands of the dominant culture. Jews are heirs of an unbroken tradition of a different concept and interpretation of God, self, community and the world sustaining an alternative identity and memory. Although the Christian culture may be unaware of Jewish self-definitions Jews have access to this cultural and religious resource. A sense of identity and the immersion in an independent culture, tradition and community, though continually beleaguered, have not been destroyed by antisemitism.

The enduring sense of Jewish identity distinguishes women's experience of sexism from Jewish men's experience of antisemitism. Since women have not been able to carry on an independent and alternative heritage, the struggle against sexist forces which undo women's names, histories and achievements has great urgency. This is equally true for Jewish women who are struggling against their invisibility in the Jewish tradition.

> The need for a feminist Judaism begins with hearing silence. It begins with noting the absence of women's history and experiences as shaping forces in the Jewish tradition. Half of Jews have been women, but men have been defined as normative Jews, while women's voices and experiences are largely invisible in the record of Jewish belief and experience that has come down to us. Women have lived Jewish history and carried its burdens, but women's perceptions and questions have not given form to scripture, shaped the direction of Jewish law, or found expression in liturgy (Plaskow 1990:1).

The place of Jewish women in the Jewish tradition is in the Background--as supporters and enablers of men. Their personhood is legally restricted (Wegner 1988), their religious role limited (Kraemer 1992:93-105) and their moral and sexual autonomy denied. Jewish women are seen as sources of pollution and deception (Fuchs 1985:137-144; Kraemer 1992:95). For Jewish women the need to counteract being *Written Out of History* (Henry and Taitz 1983) and the search for oral and written remnants of women's religious traditions are as urgent and monumental as for Gentile women. However, the recovery of Jewish women's history is further impeded by antisemitism. Consider that the Holocaust alone has wiped out two civilizations, namely Eastern European and German Jewry. The Holocaust destroyed not only places and archives but, most important, people who might have been able to tell the stories of women's traditions. Antisemitism has severely obstructed Jewish women's history.

The ideological strategies of marginalization that render oppressed groups inferior, evil and invisible should not be mistaken for similarities in the experiences of these groups. The social, political, economic and military implementation of oppression varies considerably. There are, for example, chronic violence as well as sporadic onslaughts against women (such as the witch trials) but women have never been slaughtered as indiscriminately as Jews have been in this century. But despite the Holocaust, Jews have been able to maintain their cultural memory and religious traditions. The American system of slavery, on the other hand, successfully disrupted the cultural and religious identity of African-Americans. American Blacks have not been targeted for a Holocaust, although white racism has definite genocidal traits. Similar differentiations apply to the oppression of Christian, Jewish or Black women. In other words, the similarities of the ideological underpinnings of antisemitic, racist or sexist strategies of marginalization must not be confused with actual policies and experiences of oppression.

It is important to avoid competitive claims over the primacy of antisemitism, sexism or racism. A debate about whose oppression and plight deserves greater attention (Holocaust or slavery, class or sex, sex or race) is self-defeating. A contest of suffering is vain since affliction cannot be rated and pain cannot be measured by putting them into a hierarchical order. Especially for those who suffer from multiple oppressions, sexism, antisemitism or racism are interrelated and often indistinguishable.

Bulkien points out that, "as with any politics based on a hierarchy of oppressions, the resulting schema implies that oppressions which are less `primary' are of subordinate importance and political urgency" (1984:126). She critiques Daly who dismisses antisemitism as a plausible cause for the Holocaust. Daly asserts that "the paradigm and context for genocide is trite, everyday, banalized gynocide" and maintains that one cannot grasp the "roots of evil of genocide" if one "shrinks/localizes" and tries to understand the Holocaust "strictly within ethnic and `religious group' dimensions'" (1978:311). Daly's insistence on the primacy of sexism negates the validity and power of antisemitism. Her political analysis distorts the fact that Jewish women died as Jews and not as women. The "crime" of Jewish women was being born Jewish, not being born female.

Equally flawed are the assertions of Jewish apologists who excuse sexism as a product of Judaism's adaptation to a hostile, patriarchal Gentile Christian world. These apologetic assertions bypass the fact that Jewish men, not the Gentile world, benefit from Jewish patriarchy. References to antisemitism can only partially explain the subjugation of Jewish women and their relegation to the background. By rendering antisemitism primary and sexism secondary, Jewish men ask for Jewish women to be submissive and silent. Such apologetic assertions imply that Jewish sexism would vanish once antisemitism is overcome. Similar claims have been made by other liberation movements which remained, however, patriarchal. In time, female activists in these movements were dismissed from leadership positions and confronted entrenched male supremacy as soon as the revolution was over (for Algeria see Helie-Lucas 1990:104-115).

Clearly the awareness of multiple oppressions gives feminist theologians the tools to analyze and confront antisemitism. Nevertheless, the anti-Jewish myth found its way into feminist religious writings. During the eighties Jewish feminists repeatedly raised their concerns about antisemitism in the secular and religious women's movements. Responses to these charges came from a variety of settings in the United States and West Germany.

FEMINIST ANTI-JUDAISM: THE AMERICAN DISCUSSION

American feminist discussions of anti-Judaism have taken place in three different forums: in the liberal tradition of Jewish-Christian dialogue; in historical scholarship which reconstructs women's religious voices; and in the secular women's movement which relates antisemitism to other forms of oppression, such as racism and homophobia.

Judith Plaskow and Annette Daum were among the first to voice their concerns over anti-Judaism in Christian feminist theology. As early as 1978, Plaskow's "Blaming the Jews for the Birth of Patriarchy" (1982) and Daum's "Blaming the Jews for the Death of the Goddess" (1982) focused on feminist theology and argued that Christian feminists projected Christian sexism onto Judaism in order to claim Christian origins as liberating for women. In so doing, Plaskow charged, they added "a new slant to the old theme of Christian superiority" (1982:250).

The first forum to respond to these charges did so within the parameters of Jewish-Christian dialogue (Mollenkott 1987b) which is promoted by institutions such as the National Council of Christian and Jews. In 1982 the Feminists of Faith Task Force was founded. Their philosophy reflects the premise of Jewish-Christian dialogue: "there is a unique historical relationship between Jews and Christians, and that Judaism and Christianity are two separate and distinct religious traditions. Feminists can and should have a significant role in promoting understanding and respect between Christians and Jews" (Daum and McCauley 1983:147).

In "Jewish-Christian Feminist Dialogue: A Wholistic Vision," Daum and McCauley address the community of theologians involved in Jewish-Christian dialogue as well as the feminist community. They critique Jewish-Christian dialogue because it is dominated by male elites (priests, ministers, rabbis and professors of theology who act as representatives of their communities), and excludes the majorities of the Jewish and Christian constituencies. This approach, Daum and McCauley argue, perpetuates the very structures which give rise to competition, chauvinism and mistrust between the religious traditions. They call this structure "theological triumphalism:"

> Triumphalism enshrines a pattern or system of authority within hierarchical structures which makes one class of people more important (often meaning "better than"), more powerful, and therefore more entitled to dominate than another (the authority of clergy over laity, male over female). This same system carries over to relations between institutions which vie with one another for power and dominance in relation to each other (my religious tradition over your religious tradition, my God over your God) (1983:157).

A Jewish-Christian dialogue which remains androcentric and elitist cannot fundamentally change theological triumphalism. Daum and McCauley's critique of Jewish-Christian dialogue is well taken and I agree with their assessment that only feminists who are not invested in the existing power structures can generate insights for necessary radical renewal. Since feminists have no stake in maintaining religious institutions, we have a unique opportunity for radical dialogue.

This opportunity is squandered, Daum and McCauley note, by "the problem of anti-Semitism in the women's movement and the undercurrent of anti-Judaism in feminist commentary and scholarship [which] are becoming more acute and are dividing Jewish and Christian feminists from each other" (1983:149). They argue that the feminist denunciation of Judaism, which has been present since the publication of Cady Stanton's *Woman's Bible* at the end of the last century, serves as a veiled attack on Christianity. The condemnation of sexism in Judaism functions as a substitute for the critique of Christianity--a critique which is perceived as too dangerous and threatening.

> Judaism has been the primary "Other" onto which Christianity has projected those parts of itself to which it will not lay claim. In this scenario, Judaism becomes the bad parent whom Christianity as the adult child blames and punishes for those parts of its personality it does not like and for which it refuses to accept responsibility (Daum and McCauley 1983:182).

The insight that Judaism serves as a substitute target and scapegoat will be investigated in greater detail in chapter 5. I concur with Daum and McCauley's thesis that Christian feminists absorb anti-Jewish methods and stereotypes out of ignorance and habit. Only dialogue with Jewish women enables Gentile feminists to discern and avoid anti-Jewish stereotypes.

The second forum in which anti-Judaism in Christian and neo-pagan feminist writings receives attention consists of feminists who focus on historical research. Bernadette Brooten, Ross Kraemer, Elisabeth Schüssler Fiorenza and Carol Christ have each focused on the problem of anti-Judaism in the context of historical reconstructions of Christian, Jewish and pagan women's history. Brooten and Kraemer concentrate on overcoming what Daum and McCauley have called the "Jesus was a feminist strategy" (1983:184). They do so by challenging dominant historical presuppositions and broadening the pool of evidence about Jewish women's lives in the Greco-Roman world

(Brooten 1982a, 1982b, 1982c, 1985, 1986; Kraemer 1983, 1985b, 1985c). Carol Christ proposes strategies for avoiding historical reconstructions that blame the destruction of matriarchal religions on Jewish monotheism (1987:83-93). Schüssler Fiorenza revises traditional historical hermeneutics and commits herself to an understanding and presentation of the Jesus movement as an "alternative option" rather than an "oppositional formation rejecting the values and praxis of Judaism" (1984:107). I will rely heavily on the fruits of their labors and apply the new historical information and hermeneutic principles they developed.

Finally, the third forum where feminist antisemitism is debated is in the context of the discussion of racism and other "differences" among women (for comprehensive bibliographic references, see Bulkien 1984; Klepfisz 1982:45-55; E. Beck 1982:271-277). These political and theoretical issues which arise from differences among women as a result of oppression are, without doubt, the most challenging topics for feminist theorists and activists. With Barbara Smith, I want to keep in mind that

> although all the systems of oppression cannot help but manifest themselves inside the women's movement they do not start or end there. It is fallacious and irresponsible to think that working on them internally only with other feminists is ultimately going to have a substantial, permanent effect on the power structure from which they spring (1984:84).

My investigation draws on and is indebted to the insights generated by Daum's and McCauley's analysis of androcentric triumphalism and "Othering;" Brooten's and Kraemer's historical research which alters the reconstruction of women's lives in the ancient synagogue; and, finally, the political insistence that feminist theory must become inclusive and sensitive to oppression based on criteria other than gender. My analysis of antisemitism in feminist religious writings is intended to improve feminist theology and to enlist the support of Gentile (white and Black, Christian and Goddess) feminists in the struggle against antisemitism. Until all women are free, antisemitism is as much a feminist issue as racism, classism and homophobia.

THE WEST GERMAN DISCUSSION

In contrast to the American discussion where the consciousness of anti-Judaism emerged in both secular and religious feminist movements, the German discussion focused early on religious feminist writings (Brumlik 1985, 1986; Kellenbach 1986a, 1987; Hommel 1986; Decke 1987). While the American discussion is fueled by a vibrant Jewish feminist community and feminist organizations where Jews and non-Jews collaborate (Pogrebin 1982), the German emphasis on religious writings is a legacy of the Holocaust which left the country virtually *"judenrein."* The German debate occurs *in absentia*, without ongoing input by Jewish women and men (Kellenbach 1987:46). Jewish-Christian dialogue in Germany is often carried on without Jews since only a few German-born Jews are still living in Germany, and of those, few are interested in engaging in dialogue.[5] Furthermore, in a situation where "even the word `Jew' . . . couldn't be formed by German lips [because] it was as extirpated from any German's vocabulary as were the people themselves from most of our lives after the war" (Reichel 1989:134), Christian theological writings stand out because they continue talking about Jews and Judaism. Since theologians, by and large, have not confronted antisemitism any more than the general population, religious writings are vulnerable to incorporating anti-Judaism. Like most other people in Germany, religious feminists are devoid of contacts with living Jews and rely heavily on available Christian exegetical, historical and theological sources, most of which are anti-Jewish.

Most West German feminists are part of the postwar generation and engage in feminist theological discussions outside of academic institutions. Feminist theology is developed in independent study groups among Catholic and Protestant theology students and graduate students (see Schaumberger and Massen 1986; Schaumberger 1987; Rieger 1982, 1984), the Evangelischen Akademien, Evangelischen Kirchentage and Katholikentage. The Evangelische Akademien, institutions of higher education for lay Christians, organize conferences, publish the proceedings and, thus, provide a social

---

[5] This is not to deny the influential contributions of Pinchas Lapide, Edna Brocke, Schalom Ben Chorin, Nathan Levinson and Penina Nave Levinson, David Flusser and Julius Schoeps to Jewish-Christian dialogue and of Henryk Broder, Dan Diner, Manes Sperber, Cilly Kugelmann, Lea Fleischmann, Micha Brumlik and Peter Sichrovski to Jewish-German dialogue.

context in which feminist theology is developed (see Barz 1987; Siegele-Wenschkewitz 1988, 1992:357-371). Feminist meditations on biblical texts at the Kirchentage and Katholikentage, likewise, are published as collections (Langer 1984, 1986).

The glaring absence of feminist women from German universities is another legacy of the Third Reich which successfully "disrupted" the evolution of the feminist movement and consciousness. The younger postwar generation of women had to reinvent the wheel without much support from the older generations of women. In 1985 there was "not a single woman professor on a Catholic faculty of theology in Germany, although there are a few professors on Protestant faculties" (Rieger 1985:134). Only recently have feminist, university-employed theologians, such as Marie Theres Wacker, Maria Kassel, Luise Schottroff and Helen Schlüngel-Straumann, become more visible and gained public influence in the academy. Elisabeth Moltmann-Wendel has promoted feminist theology since the early seventies. To this day, feminist theology, though gaining ground, is socially, politically, theologically and academically ostracized. Feminist theologians are severely restricted. For instance, Bernadette Brooten was dismissed from Tübingen (Blanke 1986), Elga Sorge was tried and removed from the Gesamthochschule Kassel (Olivier 1987) and Uta Ranke-Heinemann lost her teaching license (Kühn 1987). The marginalization and victimization of West German feminists has contributed to the indignation with which the issue of antisemitism has been discussed since 1986. Since feminists are a highly beleaguered and often defamed minority, there was great reluctance to accept any responsibility for anti-Judaism. Feminist theologians feared that "feminist anti-Judaism" would become a catchword to disqualify and discount them.

From the very beginning, the German feminist confrontation with anti-Judaism was charged with emotions. This is not surprising since any discussion of antisemitism threatens the very fabric of German identity. The titles of two German anthologies which responded to the charges of anti-Judaism in feminist religious writings indicate the strong linkage of the debate with the national past: *Verdrängte Vergangenheit, die uns bedrängt* [Repressed Past Which Haunts Us] (Siegele-Wenschkewitz 1988), and *Weil wir nicht vergessen wollen* [Because We Do Not Want to Forget] (Schaumberger 1987) leave no doubt about the context in which German feminists confront anti-Judaism.

The discussion of anti-Judaism shows that the definition of German
Christian feminist theology's context has to include the historical
dimension of "Auschwitz." The pains of remembering can, if we
accept them, point towards a way of seeing   the complex and
ambivalent history of women in Germany without fear and
repression (Kohn-Roelin 1987:49).

The intense and emotional atmosphere in which German feminists confront antisemitism can be compared to American feminist
controversies over racism. The cultural memories of slavery haunt and
warp the American approach to confronting racism, similar to German
discussions of antisemitism. The Holocaust perverts the very meaning
of words like "German," "Christian," "Jew" and "antisemite." Indeed,
the terms "Jew" and "antisemite" have become taboo, as if, by not
mentioning them, the integrity of what it means to be German and
Christian could be preserved. This is not unlike white America's public
image of itself as a free and democratic country which is built upon
the exploitation and oppression of African-Americans, whose very
existence is a daily reminder of America's racist and undemocratic past
and present.

A common strategy of denial among German feminists is, first,
to denounce any complicity in the terrors of Germany's antisemitic
past and, then, to avert the analysis of anti-Judaism. Most feminists
can claim the "grace of late birth" (*Gnade der späten Geburt*), as does
West Germany's chancellor Helmut Kohl, but the past defines, *nolens
volens*, the parameters of current political and theological discussions.
In light of the Holocaust, there is an overwhelming need to
disassociate oneself from any charges of anti-Judaism. A typical
defense of any German (and in this case feminist) is to issue
simultaneous declarations of guilt and innocence and to attack those
who dare to violate accepted discourse.

In one of the letters to the German feminist magazine
Schlangenbrut, which had published a series of articles addressing the
issue of anti-Judaism in feminist theology, Li Hildegardstochter
confesses her "unspeakable shame and *Schande* over the history of my
parent generation. . . I never **wanted** to, but with disgust **had to** call
myself German, and the unutterable suffering of the murdered Jews
always stood in front of my eyes" (1987:32). She then proceeds to
attack those who had raised the issue. She calls them "patriarchal and
antifeminist," whose "accusation . . . equals murder, namely character
assassination of antisemitism and racism. This is in keeping . . . with
a witch trial" (1987:32). Hildegardstochter's initial profession of guilt

and disgust frees her from the obligation to confront the past. Shame and guilt are the price she is willing to pay for disregarding the content of the charges. As Lorde formulated so poignantly (though for the American context), "all too often . . . [guilt] is just another name for impotence, for defensiveness destructive of communication; it becomes a device to protect ignorance and the continuation of things as they are, the ultimate protection for changelessness" (1984:130). The initial resistance to the realization and admission of anti-Judaism in German feminist writings points to one's emotional investment. Monika Renninger explains:

> The intensely raging discussion over criticisms of anti-Jewish tendencies in Christian feminist theology shows once more how difficult it is to abandon what one learned and became familiar with: on the one hand a much deeper than expected attachment to traditional theology, on the other hand the danger of falling back without thinking into known patterns in research and writing women's history--be it women around Jesus, Goddesses, mythological figures or witches (1987:92).

The West German discussion of anti-Judaism distinguishes itself from the American debate primarily in the emotional intensity of its denial. Without doubt, Germany's theological heritage of anti-Judaism and the legacy of the Holocaust raise the stakes.

Another idiosyncrasy of the West German discussion of anti-Judaism is its bias against neo-pagan matriarchal thealogians. Since part of the Nazi elite identified with pagan cults and rejected Christianity, there is a pervasive misperception that Christianity and Nazism were on diametrically opposed ends of the political spectrum. Though it is true that the churches resisted the Nazis on some issues (most notably the euthanasia program, cf. Lifton 1986:90-95), neither the Protestant nor Catholic churches resisted antisemitism. The popular accentuation of pagan tendencies of the Nazis and the emphasis on the secular, racist nature of their extermination policy renders Christianity more innocent and less implicated than is substantiated by evidence (see Röhm and Thierfelder 1982; Gerlach 1987). As a consequence, charges of anti-Judaism in feminist post-Christian theologies were more readily accepted since everything "pagan" was immediately linked to Nazi paganism.[6] Although it is quite ironic and politically

---

[6] A similar tendency is apparent in Ruether's attack on paganism (1980:842-847). See Budapest's response (1980:1162-1163).

dangerous when neo-pagan feminists rediscover "sacred sites" which have last been used for Nazi rituals, it is wrong to link post-Christian feminist writings with Nazi paganism. Neo-pagan feminist thealogians are no more or less predisposed to incorporate anti-Judaism than Christian feminist theologians. It is important to avoid using anti-Judaism as a political tool for disqualifying any particular feminist approach as inherently inferior.

It is only since the opening of the wall on November 8, 1989, also the anniversary of *Reichskristallnacht*, that the secular women's movement has begun to confront antisemitism and racism in its own ranks (Jacoby 1990; Hügel 1993). The rapidly declining living situation of foreign, non-white and Jewish women and men in Germany and the relative complacency of mainstream, conservative and liberal Germans have startled the women's movement into a confrontation with the problem. Whether the real threat hanging over the heads of non-white, non-Christian Germans will hasten the process of consciousness raising among white German Christians, which is required to shed longstanding stereotypes, is a question which remains to be answered. In the meantime, several of the non-Christian, non-white contributors to *Entfernte Verbindungen* [Distant Connections] have announced their decision to leave Germany, like Jewish feminist Maria Baader who begins her essay with the sentence: "This summer I will switch my place of living to New York" (1993:82).

Despite the similarities there are real differences in the presentation of Judaism in American and West German feminist theologies. While the similarities derive in part from the use of the same source materials and rootedness in the same Christian theological tradition, Germany's anti-Judaism is more deeply entrenched. It grows out of "a seamless persistence of anti-Semitic ideas in German culture over the course of the last several centuries, reaching a peak during the Third Reich" (Heschel 1993:50). It is so much part of the accepted cultural heritage that it cannot be seen for what it is and "it continues to flourish because few people recognize [antisemitic ideas] for what they are" (Heschel 1993:50). Despite frequent attestations to the contrary, Germans are deeply and emotionally invested in anti-Judaism and it is very difficult to achieve genuine change. Nevertheless, for the purposes of this book I did not distinguish a great deal between American and German feminist religious writings. While there are differences in tone and extent, the overall negative depiction and evaluation of Judaism happen on both continents. To the extent that anti- Judaism is generated by Christian theology it transcends cultural and ethnic boundaries. As I will show in my next chapter, anti-Judaism is a central Christian doctrine which shapes the representation of Judaism in Christian and post-Christian writings, American and West German theology.

Chapter II

THE TEACHING OF CONTEMPT

The Christian movement evolved out of Judaism, used Jewish terminology, competed with Jewish groups and claimed the Jewish scriptures. The early spokespeople were Jews themselves, sons and daughters of Jewish mothers and students of Jewish teachers. Judaism is therefore a constituent part of Christian discourse.

A discourse is governed by what Michel Foucault has called "rules of formation" which determine how various elements are related within a formation. Rules of formation define the elements which make up a particular discourse and the relations among those elements. They set the boundaries of a discourse and order the universe within those boundaries. Foucault explains: "By system of formation, then, I mean a complex group of relations that function as a rule: it lays down what must be related, in a particular practice, for such and such an enunciation to be made, for such and such a concept to be used and such a strategy to be organized" (1972:74).

In this chapter, "Christian theology" means the dominant tradition of Christian discourse whose rules of formation were laid down in the New Testament interpretation of the Hebrew Bible as read by the church fathers and medieval theologians, reinterpreted by the Reformers and Counter Reformers and historicized by modern biblical and theological scholarship.[1] In the following sketch of the Christian presentation of Judaism I will ignore differences between various theological traditions and focus rather on the similarities in their representation of Judaism.

---

[1] I agree with Ruether that the "anti-Judaic midrash" is rooted in the christology of the New Testament (1974a:65). Baum (1965) and Sandmel (1978) maintain that anti-Judaism is incompatible with the New Testament. See also the critique of Ruether by Meagher (1979), Idinopulos and Ward (1977).

Christian theology, of necessity, has to assign a place to Judaism within the boundaries of its discourse. The particular origin of Christianity forces every generation of theologians to evaluate anew the relation of the Old Faith (Judaism) to the New Faith (Christianity). For the most part, this evaluation of Judaism has been negative. Christian theology has rejected and repudiated Judaism and has incorporated an anti-Jewish myth as the "left hand of Christology" (Ruether 1979a:234). Anti-Judaism is a matter of Christian identity. The Christian requirement to come to terms with Judaism is not matched by an equal need on the part of Jewish theologians. They do not need to assign meaning to Christianity since Jewish identity is formed independently of the existence or nonexistence of Christianity. J. Coert Rylaarsdam illustrates:

> Judaism has constituted a far more serious problem to the Christian than Christianity to the Jew. It is internal and existential, challenging his sense of identity at the deepest level. To explain who he is the Jew need not refer to the Christian, except, perhaps, for purely practical reasons. On the other hand, the Christian finds it impossible to define himself without reference to the Jew. Christianity is a daughter faith, derivative from Judaism; and every definition of it, personal or formal, carries with it an implicit or explicit definition of Judaism. In making this inevitable definition of the Jew the Christian has assumed that because his own faith is "true" that of the Jew can be true no longer. That is his problem (1984:4).

The Christian "problem" is the problem of the later born. Consider, for example, that Christian theologians rarely ponder the theological validity of Islam. Muslim theology, on the other hand, developed an elaborate explanation for the existence of the older religions, assigning a specific place to Judaism and Christianity in its symbolic universe. The younger faith has to account for its separation from the original religion(s) and to develop its religious identity over and against the other faith(s). The older religion(s) becomes an integral part of the younger's theological discourse.

The development of Christianity as a separate, hierarchical and institutionalized religion in the first four centuries C.E. was facilitated by anti-Judaism (Efroymson 1979:100-117; Gager 1985:117-174). The "teaching of contempt" (Isaac 1964) was designed to create a unified and loyal Christian following and to defuse rival and competing Jewish truth claims (N. Beck 1985:285; Gager 1985:117-134). Anti-Judaism elucidated Christianity's continuity with the Jewish past and emphasized its difference and discontinuity from the "Old Israel." At the same time, Christian theology disqualified Judaism by presenting the Jewish religious leadership and, later, the entire people as "Christ-killers."

I propose that the distorted representation of Judaism in Christianity is governed by three rules of formation. The first rule of formation depicts Judaism as the **antithesis** of Christian beliefs and values. It identifies Judaism with the negative side of dualistic oppositions such as "justice and love," "judgment and promise" or "law and grace." While the definitions of Christianity change, Judaism is always correlated as its opposite. By rendering Judaism its negative antithesis, Christian theology asserts its difference and superiority over the rival faith.

The second rule of formation is closely related to the first because it builds on negative characterizations of Judaism. Christian theology casts Israel into the role of **scapegoat** and characterizes Jews as guilty, evil and predisposed to "deicide." Israel is blamed for evil in the world. As a punishment for her various crimes culminating in Christ's murder, Israel is rejected by God who elects the Gentile church instead as the legitimate heir of Israel's covenant with God. The portrayal of Jews as morally depraved, politically sinister and religiously ominous legitimates Christianity's replacement of Israel.

The third rule of formation misrepresents Judaism as old and outdated. This rule of formation accounts for Christianity's continuity with Israel's past by reducing Judaism to the status of a **prologue** of Christianity. Judaism is identified with the "Old" Testament and seen as a relic of ancient times rather than as a contemporary and vital religious alternative. As a result, Judaism can legitimately be incorporated as Christian prehistory.

These rules of formation operate simultaneously and govern the perception of Judaism in the Christian mind. This may account for the continuity--not sameness--of the anti-Jewish myth throughout different centuries, countries, cultures and world views. These rules of formation of the teaching of contempt have moved beyond the realm of theological discourse and have guided the secularized, economic, political and racist myths of the Jews since the 19th century.[2] For instance, the left-wing myth asserts that the Jews are an anachronistic religious and national group (prologue), opposed to universal egalitarianism and internationalism (antithesis) and responsible for the introduction of trade and money economy through their practice of usury (scapegoat). The right-wing myth, on the other hand, maintains that the Jews are an inferior, uncivilized race (prologue), who undermine national pride and champion liberal internationalism (antithesis) and are responsible for the creation of Bolshevik communist theory and practice (scapegoat). While the specific content of anti-Judaism shifts drastically, the rules of formation of the anti-Jewish discourse remain the same. It is the power of anti-Judaism to adapt to the specific needs of particular countries, classes and political groups. Building on the work of scholars in the Jewish-Christian dialogue I will delineate representations of Judaism as antithesis, scapegoat and prologue in Christian theological discourse which will clarify the particular shifts which occur in the representation of Judaism in feminist Christian-rooted writings.

ANTITHESIS

Several scholars have pointed out the detrimental effects of dualistic thinking on Jewish-Christian relations. In her pioneering work, *Faith and Fratricide*, Rosemary Radford Ruether argues that the Christian understanding of Judaism is shaped by three dichotomies, namely "judgment and promise," "particularism and universalism" and "letter and spirit" (1974a:226-256). Christianity, she contends, appropriates the "positive" side of these dualistic oppositions and identifies the "negative" side of judgment, particularism and letter with Judaism.

> These dualisms, which make Judaism their negative side, are so deeply ingrained in Christian language that modern critical theology and liberal sermonizing still remain largely oblivious to their implications. . . . These antitheses, presumed to be an accurate

---

[2] Alan Davies presents a good review of various positions concerning the continuity and/or discontinuity of religious anti-Judaism with secular racist antisemitism (1979:188-208). For a socio-historical analysis of the differences between 19th century political and religious antisemitism, see Uriel Tal 1971, 1975.

description of Judaism, both then and now, remain a basic mode of
Christian thinking and preaching (1974a:228-229).

Dualistic thinking divides the world into opposites and elevates
one side above the other. A dualistic opposition such as "particularism
and universalism" creates a false image of reality because it conceals
the particularity of Christianity and disguises its particular cultural and
religious customs, doctrines and beliefs as universal truths. It also
denies universal elements within Judaism. But even more troublesome
are the value judgments which accompany these divisions. "In a
dualistic praxis, `the other' is always better or worse, more or less,
than oneself or one's people. Identity is forged and known by contrast
and competition, not by cooperative relation" (Heyward 1989:18). In
the dichotomy of universalism and particularism, universalism is
assigned greater value while particularism is denigrated. Thus, Judaism
is perceived not only as the opposite of Christianity (rather than as a
religion in its own right) but is simultaneously devalued.

Dualistic thinking creates self-confidence and a sense of
importance and superiority by maintaining the inferiority of an Other.
By comparing itself with an inferior Other, Christianity appears to
have greater faith, a purer spirituality and a superior revelation.
Virginia Woolf has observed how the dualistic construction of gender
serves men by making women into "looking glasses possessing the
magic and delicious power of reflecting the figure of man at twice its
natural size" (1957:35). Christianity uses Judaism in a similar way.
Judaism becomes a repository of Christianity's own unacknowledged
negative traits. By looking into the mirror Christianity reassures itself
of what it is not. Continual antithetical comparisons with a negative
image become a necessary process for Christian construction of
identity. The comparison with an inferior Other confirms Christianity's
perception of itself as a vibrant, revolutionary, future-oriented, young
movement which opposes a degenerated, rigid, lifeless, narrow,
legalistic and bureaucratic tradition. Thus, Christianity proves its
theological superiority and legitimacy.

Furthermore, as the primordial Other, Judaism assumes the
characteristics of various opponents in Christian history. For instance,
the Reformers fused the Catholic position with the Jews and used the
New Testament conflict between Jesus and the Jews as a theological
tool to repudiate the Catholic church. As a result, the Protestant
representation of Judaism has adopted some of the traits of
Catholicism, such as "the existence of a treasury of merits established

by works of supererogation. We have here the retrojection of the
Protestant-Catholic debate into ancient history, with Judaism taking the
role of Catholicism and Christianity the role of Lutheranism" (Sanders
1977:57; see also Gager 1985:31-34). The antithetical role of Judaism
is utilized for inner-Christian conflicts and, as a result, Judaism
acquires the negative characteristics of succeeding opponents.

I want to draw attention to three areas of profound rethinking
as a result of Jewish-Christian dialogue: the reassessment of the
religious diversity of Judaism during the period of the Second Temple,
the identity and role of the Pharisees and the nature of Jewish law.

Klein's *Anti-Judaism in Christian Theology* documents that a
majority of European Christian exegetes, religious historians and
theologians maintain that Israelite religion declined in the period of the
Second Temple (515 B.C.E.- 70 C.E.) (1978:15-39). This historical
reconstruction of "late Judaism" as a dry, lifeless and faithless religion
drifting towards spiritual extinction is challenged and revised. Scholars
committed to overcoming anti-Judaism are beginning to understand the
period from 200 B.C.E. to 200 C.E. as a time of creative chaos where
the challenges of a "New Age" were met by a variety of religious,
political and philosophical groups and where the "Jewish Way" and
the "Christian Way" (Van Buren 1980) developed as two equally
valid, albeit competing, truth claims (Rendtorff 1980:99-116;
1981:332-347; Lacocque 1968:120-143). Jewish history emerges in a
rich diversity "which can be explained by religious and intellectual
vitality rather than as symptomatic of confusion and disorientation"
(Blenkinsopp 1980:111). The previous antithetical contrasts between
the "new, vital, revolutionary Jesus movement" and the "old, stale,
dying Judaism" are dismantled by research which exposes these
contrasts as christocentric fiction (Fuchs-Kreimer 1981:80).

The anti-Jewish notion of Israel's religious decline provided
"historical evidence" for the depiction of Jesus' Jewish environment as
inferior. As Nancy Fuchs-Kreimer points out, this understanding is in
part suggested by the New Testament depiction of the Pharisees as
legalistic, calculating and narrow-minded. The New Testament polemic
profoundly influences the Christian antithetical perception of Judaism.
According to the Gospels, the Pharisees ask trick questions of Jesus,
raise incessant objections to his actions, complain about his
transgressions of the law, blame him for his dealings with sinners and
quarrel about matters of food, the Sabbath, divorce and forgiveness of
sins. The Pharisees emerge as elitist, arrogant, self-righteous,
hypocritical and advocates of a double-standard. Intent on preserving

their elite status, the Pharisees are looking for ways to eliminate Jesus which eventually lead to his death. Their contempt for ordinary people has become proverbial.

In recent years, scholars have challenged this depiction on historical grounds and pointed out that of all religious groups the Pharisees were theologically closest to the Jesus movement. Instead of being Jesus' archenemies, the Pharisees espoused similar beliefs. They introduced the concept of "oral Torah," which allowed them to radically change and reform the "written Torah." They believed in bodily resurrection from the dead; they advocated the democratization of religious leadership and limited the religious authority of the Temple priests; they internalized spirituality and individualized the relation of the believer to God. Resisting the pitfalls of the first rule of formation, scholars point out that the polemics of the New Testament arise precisely because the two movements were theologically compatible and, during Jesus' lifetime, hard to distinguish. In their assessment the Pharisees were powerful competitors of the early church.[3] As the precursors of Rabbinic Judaism, they engaged in a radical transformation of Judaism. After the destruction of the Temple in 70 C.E., they forged the new identity of Israel outside the land of Israel, without government, without Temple, without military power. The creation of Judaism as we know it must be credited to the Pharisees. It was a revolution which occurred simultaneously with the Christian revolution, and it was this rival creativity which triggered the New Testament polemics against the Pharisees (Rivkin 1978).

The rule of formation of antithesis prevents this realization from penetrating mainstream theology where Pharisaic religion continues to be described as oppressive and spiritually void:

> This law, which ruled the life of the Jew in an abundance of individual precepts and prohibitions, was no longer understood as God's living word but had become a rigid, firmly outlined factor. . . . The law involves the greatest threat which can seize on man: the desire to boast before God of success attained by one's own strength, in virtue of the law, in fulfilling and mastering one's life (Lohse quoted in Klein 1978:54).

---

[3] For research on the Pharisees that emphasizes similarities between the Jesus movement and the Pharisees: Rivkin 1978; Neusner 1971; Cook 1978:441-460; Pawlikowski 1982:76-108; Ruether 1974a:53-64; Williamson 1982; Swidler 1981:104-114, 1988; Thoma 1980. For an opposing view, see Sigal 1987.

For Lohse, the Jewish follower of Torah is cursed either because the Law cannot be fulfilled or because fulfilling the Law leads to arrogance and pride. Arrogance, pride and the inability to admit human inadequacy and sinfulness before God explain the Jewish "No" to Christ. The reductionist portrayal of Judaism as legalism is deeply ingrained in Protestant theology, continually reaffirmed by the Gospels' depiction of the Pharisees and by traditional readings of Paul's opposition to "works of law" (Gal 2:16-3:14; Rom 3:20-4:25). Rabbinic sources are often used selectively to enhance Paul's polemic against "works of the law" and to create the impression of a religion where individuals save themselves by strict, unfeeling and unthinking obedience to a body of laws (Moore 1921:191-254).[4] The Judaism which emerges is thoroughly unappealing, oppressive and pointless.

> The frequent Christian charge against Judaism, it must be recalled, is not that some individual Jews misunderstood, misapplied and abused their religion, but that **Judaism necessarily tends** towards petty legalism, self-serving and self-deceiving casuistry, and a mixture of arrogance and lack of confidence in God (Sanders 1977:427).

Jewish "legalism" and "work-righteousness" form the background against which Christian teaching and identity establish themselves. The Pharisees and Jewish law are used as a foil to enhance the Christian message as a superior faith experience. Since the New Testament is more than a historical text, the confrontation between "Christian" and "Jewish" values provides a conflict paradigm for Christians who read, hear and interpret the New Testament and who experience themselves in opposition to something or somebody in their own specific environments. The Jews become symbols of opposition, a projection screen which can be filled with the particular opponents confronting particular Christians. In chapters 3 to 5 I will document the ways in which Christian and neo-pagan feminist writings apply this antithetical conflict paradigm and identify Judaism with the patriarchal opponent.

---

[4] For reinterpretations of Paul in the context of Jewish-Christian dialogue, see Stendahl 1976; Gaston 1979, 1986; Sanders 1977; Barth 1968:78-104; 1977:45-134; Gager 1985:193-247; Williamson 1982:47-64; Osten-Sacken 1982.

SCAPEGOAT

Scapegoating occurs when human beings cannot bear ambiguity but idealize themselves, their community or beliefs.[5] The purity of a group or doctrine is maintained by projecting unwelcome aspects onto an Other. Ruether argues that the Christian emphasis on realized redemption creates the need to project unredeemed aspects in the church, evil and sin onto an outsider (Ruether 1974a:226-257 and Pawlikowski's response 1979:151-167). Ruether identifies several "strange bedfellows" who have traditionally been made into scapegoats.

> Since the church, at least objectively and institutionally, represented the completion of Christ's salvation, blame for collective evil tended to be externalized. The Christians tended to project the causes of evil outward, locating it in a demonic "conspiracy" surrounding the people of God, which was personified in religious or social aliens, in heretics, or in the revolt in the "flesh," i.e. serfs, women, beneath its "head." Women and Jews for centuries were two scapegoats of this paranoid tendency of Christian culture (1975:109).

Judaism has become a symbol of evil. The deicide charge which has been repeated on Good Fridays in churches all over the world has made the Jew of central symbolic importance for the Christian drama of salvation. As *Sacred Executioners* (Maccoby 1983), the Jew symbolizes the Christian's own sins for which Christ died. "The eternal Jew (`der ewige Jude') becomes a guarantee of the permanence of the salvation afforded by the Crucifixion; as long as the Jew continues his mysteriously prolonged existence in suffering, the Christian can feel assured of salvation" (Maccoby 1983:142). Through their participation in deicide, Jews take upon themselves God's wrath and serve as perpetual reminders of God's punishment for those who stray from the path of righteousness.

Although the statement, "the Jews killed Jesus" makes as much sense as the statement "the Americans killed Kennedy" (Eckardt 1974:12; Williamson 1982:45), it continues to be

---

[5] Scapegoat theories are employed by sociologists and psychoanalysts trying to understand violent impulses/outbursts in and between communities: Allport on racism (1985), Muchemblad on witch hunts (1979:271), Simmel on antisemitism (1946). For a good critique of scapegoat theories, see Sallen 1977:88ff.

a commonplace, despite all attempts--even those of the Second Vatican Council--to introduce less sweeping statements and to explain the circumstances at the time. Despite doubts about the historical accuracy of the account of the trial before the Sanhedrin, most theologians continue to maintain their former view of an irreconcilable hostility between Jesus and the Jews. This hostility is then seen as leading logically to his death (Klein 1978:92).

Other research on the events leading up to Jesus' death concludes that two fatal shifts characterize the Christian perception of the role of Jews in the death of Jesus. First, the responsibility for the death of Jesus is shifted from Roman colonial powers to Jewish authorities. Secondly, the religious charge, namely blasphemy, is added to the political indictment against Jesus for claiming to be the "Rex Iudeaorum," King of the Jews, presumably on the suspicion of rebellion against the Roman imperial government (Brandon 1968). Numerous inconsistencies and contradictions in the Gospel accounts of the last days of Jesus give evidence to these shifts (Cohn 1967). Many theologians uncritically embrace the Gospels' shift of "blame for the death of Jesus and his disciples from Roman political authority to Jewish religious authority" (Ruether 1974a:88). For many Christians, Jesus was convicted for blasphemy and related religious reasons while Pontius Pilate was coaxed and tricked into a conviction. Pontius Pilate, though historically known for his brutality as governor of Palestine, was sometimes celebrated as a secret Christian and even sanctified by the Ethiopian church (Brandon 1968:155; Bratton 1969:30). The Jewish religion, on the other hand, is blamed for the death of Christ.

The deicide charge holds all Jews accountable for the death of Christ. It is a collective guilt which taints every Jew in the past, present and future. Jewish guilt is extended backwards and the people of Israel are charged with a long record of crimes and endowed with an essentially evil character. Israel's history is presented as a "trail of crimes" (Ruether 1974a:124ff). The Jews are described as idolaters (Ex 32) who committed incest and sexual perversions, were gluttons and succumbed easily to many vices. Israel always ignored those sent by God, persecuted and even killed the prophets. They were obstinate, blind, disobedient. Indeed, the devil is their father and "the lusts of your father you will do. He was a murderer from the beginning" (Jn 8:44). This trail of crimes symbolically prepares the Jews for their role as sacred executioners. Klein's collection of respectable theologians who embrace the myth of Jewish evil is remarkable. Heinrich Schlier may suffice:

There is an undercurrent of hostility to God running right through the history of Israel in the Old Testament from generation to generation. And it was finally concentrated in deadly hatred against him in whom God--who gives everything --pressed hard on Israel. . . . It is this blindness which fills their history with such great self-consciousness, unrest, resentment and fanaticism (quoted in Klein 1978:109).

Although many churches have taken steps since the Holocaust to repudiate the deicide charge (Croner 1977), the scapegoating of Jews for Christ's death still occurs. The power of the deicide charge originates in the christological doctrine that "Christ died for our sins." The charge that he was crucified by the Jews relieves the Christian of that burden. Eugene Fisher warns:

To the extent that we continue to project our own responsibility as sinners away from ourselves and on to "the Jews," to that extent do we obscure and even pervert the religious challenge to ourselves of the Pascal mystery. We enter this mystery of the faith by acknowledging our sinfulness and responsibility. To project the drama, unhistorically and falsely, unto "the Jews," is to remove ourselves from participation in the death and therefore in the resurrection of Jesus (1984:426).

The existence of the Jewish scapegoat enables Christians to identify with the innocent victim.[6] While Christians are symbolically represented by Christ, the Jews are cast as powerful agents who can be held accountable for their actions. The victim, Jesus, and by extension, the Christian, is powerless and has no moral guilt. The sacrificial lamb is pure and innocent. By identifying with the sacrificial lamb, Christian theology often deprives itself of theological mechanisms to understand itself as perpetrator and powerful agent. Despite two thousand years of Christian rule and domination Christians regularly perceive themselves as innocent and powerless

---

[6] Sociologist Allport suggests that "symbolically, therefore, sinful Christians are also `Christ killers.' But this thought is so painful that it must be repressed" (1985:249). Psychoanalyst Loewenstein argues in his classic *Christians and Jews* that "the function of anti-Semitism has been that of a displacement and projection of their [i.e. Gentile Christian] unconscious revolt against Christ, while keeping their love for Christ intact on a conscious level" (1951:100). For Eckardt antisemitism is an unconscious revolt of Gentile Christians against the Jewishness of Jesus and of God. The deicide charge is an unconscious death wish for Christ, perceived by Christians as a Jewish wish to kill Christ. This death can be satisfied by killing Jews as substitute victims for Jesus (1974:87-90).

like Jesus and place Judaism and Jews in the role of powerful perpetrators.

The correlation of Judaism with power and evil enjoys a longstanding literary, theological, artistic, legal and political tradition. In medieval literature, the Jew acquires sensuous and carnal traits and is routinely associated with the devil and/or Antichrist. Fantastic ingenuity merges the worship of the golden calf with the mysterious dietary laws which are supposedly given by God to restrain the Jews' depraved appetites. The blood libel (accusation of the slaughter of Christian babies to bake matzo for Passover) instills fear and fury and regularly leads to pogroms. In Christian lore and the arts the devil, the Antichrist and various pagan and demonic forces wear Jewish faces and are characterized by Jewish names and attributes. For centuries, the Jews have lurked behind every disease, famine, war, heresy, unrest and injustice: from the Black Death (poisoning of wells) to mysterious Jewish influences which supposedly caused the Reformation, Enlightenment, liberalism, communism and capitalism. Judaism becomes indispensable as a symbol of evil.

The a priori guilt of Jews and their association with the devil has been passed on to modern racist conceptions of Jews as a contagious and dangerous threat to the health of the *Volk*. Trachtenberg concluded his massive study *The Devil and The Jews* in 1943: "Antisemitism today is `scientific'; it would disdain to include in the contemporaneous lexicon of Jewish crime such outmoded items as satanism and sorcery. . . . To the modern antisemite, of whatever persuasion, the Jew has become the international communist or the international banker, or better, both. But his aim is still to destroy Christendom, to conquer the world and to enslave it to his own--and the word is inescapable--devilish ends" (1983:219).

The rule of formation of scapegoat creates suspicion and mistrust towards Jews and Judaism. The myth of Jewish history as a trail of crimes continually seeks and finds validation and meticulously searches out any Jewish involvement in cheating, exploiting, controlling, spying and oppressing. At the same time, the perpetuation of the myth suppresses all evidence to the contrary. Chapter 6 will analyze the extent to which this myth of Jewish evil has entered feminist religious writings and influences the feminist Christian and post-Christian presentation of Judaism.

PROLOGUE

Christian theology claims to participate in Israel's story with God who elected, liberated and promised peace, justice and redemption to Israel. Christianity's continuity with this ancient past proved to be vitally important in the Roman world which valued tradition and antiquity highly. Gager argues that the claim to Israel's past was an essential ingredient in the church's success and "that the elements in Judaism that appealed to educated pagans--great antiquity, written scriptures, sense of morality, monotheism--are precisely those things that Christianity will emphasize as it presents itself as the `true Israel' to the very same audience" (1985:66). Christian theology annexes Judaism as its **prologue** and renders Judaism outdated. Judaism becomes identified with the "Old" Testament, judged as antiquated and superseded by the New Testament which absorbs, incorporates and eventually leaves the former behind. The old ceases to exist. Martin Noth, for instance, ends his *History of Israel* in the first century:

> Jesus himself, with his words and his work, no longer formed part of the history of Israel. In him the history of Israel had come, rather, to its real end. What did belong to the history of Israel was the process of his rejection and condemnation by the Jerusalem religious community. It had not discerned in him the goal to which the history of Israel had secretly been leading; it rejected him as the promised Messiah. Only a few had joined him, and from them something new proceeded. The Jerusalem religious community imagined it had more important concerns, and kept aloof from this new movement. Hereafter the history of Israel moved quickly to its end (quoted in Klein 1978:26).

Israel's history ends because all of God's promises and prophecies are transferred to the Gentile church, the newly elect people of God. The old "carnal" Israel loses its privileges and is dismissed. Matthew's parables of the vineyard (22:33-44), the wedding meal (22:1-7) and the new wineskins (9:17) set up the supersessionist paradigm. These parables show that the inheritance of the Father, or the invitation by the Lord, will be turned over from bad guardians and ungrateful guests to undeserving but trusting and faith-ful newcomers. The church fathers see the disinheritance of Israel and the election of the Gentiles foreshadowed and predicted in the Hebrew Bible:

> It is prefigured and foretold in the ancient heroes and prophets. .
> .. The Jews assume the status of a people on probation who fail
> all the tests and finally are flunked out. The message of election
> refers to a believing people. The Jews proved through their history
> that they are not this people. So the believing people becomes a
> historical reality only with the Gentile church (Ruether 1974a:135).

The theology of replacement denies the validity of the Jewish religion and negates Israel's right to exist. Israel is rejected by God and punished for deicide. Israel is dispersed among the nations, the Temple destroyed, the land devastated and the people forced into exile as a consequence of their obstinacy and blindness. Martin Noth contends that "the descendants of the Israel of old had become strangers in their former homeland just as they were in the Diaspora; and their holy city was prohibited to them. Thus ended the ghastly epilogue of Israel's history" (quoted in Klein 1978:26). The alleged expulsion from the land of Israel into exile and misery is of vital theological importance because it "proves" the divine invalidation of Israel's election and covenant (Isaac 1964:39-69). Homelessness, eternal foreignism and restless wandering substantiate that God's promises to Israel are void. Fourth-century poet Prudentius describes this situation: "From place to place the homeless Jew wanders in ever-shifting exile, since the time when he was torn from the abode of his fathers and has been suffering the penalty for murder and having stained his hands with the blood of Christ" (quoted in Ruether 1974a:134).

The intimate connection between Israel's exile and Christianity's truth claim to be the newly elected people of God is apparent in Martin Luther's *Wider die Sabbather an einen guten Freund*. For him, the return of the Jewish people to the land of Israel would prove the continuing validity of the Old Covenant. Should this event come about, a possibility he simply could not imagine, he promised that Christians would convert to Judaism:

> [L]et them [the Jews] head for Jerusalem, build temples, set up
> priesthood, principalities, Moses with his laws, and in other words
> themselves become Jews again and take the land into their
> possession. For when this happens, they will see us [Christians]
> quickly on their heels and likewise become Jews. But if not, then
> it is entirely ludicrous that they should want to persuade us into
> accepting their degenerate laws, which are surely by now after
> 1500 years of decay no longer laws at all. And should we believe
> what they themselves do not and cannot believe, as long as they do

not have Jerusalem and the land of Israel? (quoted in Oberman 1981:64, n.137).

One wonders how much Christian anti-Zionism is rooted in the fear that a Jewish state proves the continuing validity of Judaism. Christians fiercely opposed the rebuilding of the Temple suggested by the Roman Emperor Julian in 362 C.E. (Marcus 1981:8-12), and stripped the comfortable and well-respected Jewish community of their previously held civil rights in the Roman Empire (Isaac 1964:39-69, 1971:89-94). Once Christianity became the official religion of the state, the legislative and military power of the Roman Empire transformed the theology of replacement into social reality.

In 339 C.E., Emperor Constantine imposed capital punishment on Jewish attempts to missionize after some of his workers converted to Judaism (see Brooten 1982c:146). The conversion of slaves to Judaism had already been prohibited in 325. In 351, the Gallic governor burned a Torah scroll. In 357, a new law was passed mandating that the property of a Christian who converted to Judaism be confiscated. Julian (361-381) known as "the Apostate," eased the pressure on the Jewish community and actively protected it from Christian persecution. He was chastised by St. Ambrosius when he permitted the rebuilding of a synagogue which had been burned down by Christians. Beginning in 408 until 450, Jews were prohibited from building new synagogues and keeping Christian slaves. In 415, Cyril, bishop of Alexandria, incited a Christian mob to expel the Jews of Alexandria. This was the first expulsion in a long miserable history of expulsions of Jews from Christian lands.[7] The theological motif of homelessness and wandering was enforced by a systematic policy of deprivation of rights until Jews were legally forced into the status of foreigners under special protection and subject to special taxes.[8] They could no longer own land or slaves, or employ servants. Instead, they themselves became serfs of the chamber, the private property of feudal lords (Parkes 1976).

---

[7] Grosser and Halperin present a concise overview of antisemitic laws and incidents (1979).

[8] This was particularly true for Northern Europe. Mediterranean countries were less effective in turning Jews into foreigners. All the more traumatic was the expulsion of Jews from Spain in 1492. For histories of the Jews in Europe, see Poliakov 1965-1976; Baron 1969 Vol. XIII; Parkes 1974, 1976; Heer 1967; and Jeremy Cohen 1982.

As prologue, Israel becomes an anachronism in the Christian universe. Christian seminaries rarely teach Jewish history, thought or religion beyond the destruction of the Second Temple. Judaism becomes invisible as a contemporary alternative because it poses a threat to Christianity's claim to possess the sole truth. After all, Judaism presents an alternative reading of the Hebrew Bible. Throughout Christian history, followers of alternative (read pagan or heretical) expressions of spirituality were persecuted and killed, their books burned and destroyed. Judaism fared a little better until modern times. In contrast to pagan and heretical movements, Israel was allowed to survive because it testified to the truth of the Bible and because the church believed that a remnant of Israel would convert at the end of times upon Christ's triumphant return. In the meantime, Jews were tolerated as living proofs of God's punishment for non-believers.

It was the Holocaust and the establishment of the state of Israel that jolted Christian theologians into the realization that Israel still exists despite Christian claims to the contrary. The near complete annihilation of European Jewry and the establishment of Jewish self-government in the land of Israel called for a rethinking of traditional Christian claims. Several Catholic as well as Protestant theologians acknowledged the continuing existence of Israel and began to develop a theological basis for the acceptance of Judaism as a religious alternative. These theologians endeavor to formulate a new Christian understanding of covenant which does not deny or invalidate the ongoing covenant of Israel with God (McGarry 1982). One school of scholars proposes the existence of two distinct yet equal covenants, while another school maintains that Christianity and Judaism share one basic covenant with the God of Israel, but fulfill different tasks within this covenant. Ruether, a "two covenant theologian," suggests the existence of two distinct "paradigms of revelation" which she calls Sinai and Calvary (1974:239-257). E.P. Sanders, another "two-covenant theologian," understands Judaism and Christianity as two distinct "patterns of religion," namely, "covenantal nomism" and "participationist eschatology" (1977:422, 549). "Single covenant theologians," such as Van Buren, Eckardt and Hellwig maintain that Christians are invited as Gentiles into Israel's covenant with God through Christ. Van Buren contends that "the Way of Israel" remains valid and separate from "the Way of the Church," although "our movement along the Way, together with Israel, is for the sake and itself part of God's plan and purpose for His whole creation" (1980:

48). Jewish conversion to the Christian Way is discouraged as Gentiles are challenged to accept the primacy of Israel's Way with God and to understand their "particular identity as Gentiles in the Way" (1980:26).

These theological revisions of covenant intend to rescind the rule of formation of prologue which renders Judaism invisible as a contemporary religious alternative. These scholars oppose the marginalization of Jewish history and thought and call for the rediscovery of Jewish learning. Ruether warns that the "very suppression of Jewish history and experience from Christian consciousness is tacitly genocidal" (1974a:258). In chapter 7 I will examine whether feminists heed these calls or continue to present Judaism as old and outdated.

The rules of formation are used as guidelines to group and categorize certain distortions and stereotypes. A rule of formation is not necessarily the origin of a specific distortion but rather indicates the position of Judaism within a Christian theological discourse. Anti-Jewish distortions occur because Judaism is cast into the roles of antithesis, scapegoat and prologue in Christian discourse.

Chapter III

JUDAISM

AS ANTITHESIS OF EARLY CHRISTIANITY

In this chapter I will examine the widespread perception that Jewish women's social position at the time of Jesus was exceedingly low and that Jesus' attitude towards women differed radically from his Jewish male contemporaries. This emphasis on the oppression of Jewish women during the Hellenistic Age serves to accentuate the visibility, equality and dignity of early Christian women. It is based upon biased and selective readings of historical materials of the New Testament as well as rabbinic and Greco-Roman sources which emphasize the subordination of Jewish women in order to highlight Jesus' exceptional treatment of women. As Bernadette Brooten points out (1986:65-91), this contrast relies in part on exegetical and historical studies of "women's status" prepared by (German) scholars who were both sexist and anti-Jewish, such as Johannes Leipoldt, Georg Oepke, Joachim Jeremias and Friedrich Heiler.

It is particularly noteworthy that these four German scholars published their research on women during the Holocaust. Johannes Leipoldt, notorious for his antisemitism, published a treatise on *Antisemitismus in der antiken Welt* in 1933, which is a classic example of the successful union of Christian anti-Judaism with racist antisemitism. In 1938, he joined the *Institut zur Erforschung des jüdischen Einflusses auf das kirchliche Leben*, whose stated goal was the elimination of Jewish influences from church life. "These theologians rejected the Old Testament, proclaimed an Aryan rather than a Jewish Jesus, and fused pagan and Christian elements into a peculiarly German mysticism" (Ericksen 1985:48). After 1945, Leipoldt's thinking on antisemitism did not change as evident in his article in the *Reallexikon für Antike und Christentum* (1950:470-475). Unfortunately, Leipoldt was also interested in the "woman question" and wrote two widely used books on women in the ancient world and the early church, *Die Frau in der antiken Welt und im Urchristentum* (1955) and *Jesus und die Frauen* (1921).[1]

Oepke first became interested in women in 1939, when he wrote "Der Dienst der Frau in der urchristlichen Gemeinde" (1939:39-53). Another article (1957) continues to be reprinted in English in such standard works as the abridged version of the *Theological Dictionary to the New Testament* (1985:134-136). Friedrich Heiler published his first article on women in world religions in 1939, while Joachim Jeremias appended his research on women to *Jerusalem zur Zeit Jesu* (1962) in 1938 under the general heading, "The Purity of the *Volkstum.*" The dates of publication alone should preclude any uncritical use of this research. Although these scholars purport to give a historically objective account of women's status in Judaism, Christianity and Hellenism, they were in fact arguing Christian (in Leipoldt's case, Aryan) supremacy and chose their material accordingly. By selecting certain "details about the rights, duties, privileges, disabilities, options and restrictions that the women of a specific group experience" (Hackett 1985:17), they introduced anti-Jewish interpretations. Their historical and exegetical studies were guided by a theological agenda of Christian supremacy. By relying on these studies, feminist theologians incorporate their bias.

THE UN-JEWISHNESS OF JESUS

Feminist approaches to Jesus emphasize his uniqueness and stress that his attitudes towards women were unparalleled and unprecedented. Jesus' views and actions are characterized as "puzzling" (Ruether 1983:5), "striking" (Daly 1985a:78), "extraordinary" (S. Collins 1974:129), "unconventional and astonishing" (Stagg and Stagg 1978: 116), "revolutionary" (Sorge 1985:24) "totally different" (Wolff 1979: 80), a "radical break" (Jewett 1975:95), "radically shocking to his contemporaries" (Mollenkott 1977:19), "rejections of his contemporary norms and customs" (Grant 1989:103) and "very different from his peers" (Swidler 1979:352; cf. Ruether 1975:63-65; Russell 1974:87; Moltmann-Wendel 1977:12,18; Gray 1994:28-36). This appraisal of Jesus as a unique and exceptional figure requires historical renditions of the New Testament which depict Jesus as a man who

---

[1] Pagels, for example, bases her evaluation of Paul on Leipoldt (1979:73).

stood apart from and over against his religious Jewish environment. Theologians committed to Jesus' historical uniqueness select historical data about Second Temple Judaism in a way which highlights and dramatizes differences and contrasts between Jesus and Judaism. Jesus' liberal attitudes towards women are not presented as typical for certain sectors of Judaism but as antithetical to Jewish sexism and patriarchy.

Some Christian feminist descriptions of Jewish patriarchy rely on a selection of laws, customs, behaviors and conventions including some or all of the following: Women are said to be legally, religiously, socially and economically subjected to men. They are not to be seen or heard in public. They are not counted in the *Minyan*, the quorum of ten males required for religious services, and are excluded from active participation in the synagogue. Men are not allowed to speak with women or visit their houses unless a male family member is present. Women may not serve men at the table. The Jewish woman is veiled as a sign of her submission, silence and sub-ordination. Women are generally uneducated and prevented from studying Torah. They are considered property of men, to be given away in arranged marriages by fathers and taken care of by husbands or brothers of dead husbands. They may be divorced at any time for no reason while they cannot divorce men. Men can marry several wives and are not legally responsible for adultery unless they violate another man's property by having sexual relations with a married woman. Women's virginity must be guarded at all costs. Women's sexuality is considered dangerous and polluting, and women are declared unclean during menstruation and after childbirth. During times of impurity women are segregated and socially ostracized. According to these descriptions, contempt for women reached a high point at the time of Jesus.

Against this cultural and religious backdrop, Jesus' treatment of women appears liberating: Jesus talks to women, visits their homes, defends, touches and heals women. Jesus allows women to follow and serve him and to discuss theology with him. To be sure, none of Jesus' actions would qualify him as a feminist in our time: Jesus never demanded that restrictive laws be dismantled or that women be allowed to become apostles and missionaries. Cynthia Ozick's observation about the Torah's missing commandment, "Thou shalt not lessen the humanity of women!" (1983:149) is confirmed by a similar *lacuna* in the New Testament. Jesus does not speak out explicitly against the oppression of women. Yet, when Jesus' reticence is viewed antithetically against the background outlined above a different interpretation becomes possible.

For instance, after a two page expose on the Jewish treatment of women Virginia Mollenkott concludes that "the more we find out about the cultural conditions of Rabbinic Judaism, the more we realize that . . . Jesus was deliberately breaking rabbinic customs that were degrading to the self-concept of women" (1977:13). If Jesus is seen against the backdrop of a severely restrictive society, he can be depicted as someone opposed to sexist oppression. If one argues that public conversations between men and women were prohibited in Israel, one can claim that Jesus broke the law when he engaged in discussions with women, deliberately transgressing restrictive gender conventions.[2] By implication, he appears as a supporter of women's rights. If, however, there were no laws against speaking to women a deliberate egalitarianism on Jesus' part would be less striking. If men and women mixed freely in the land of Israel Jesus' behavior would not be revolutionary. Without doubt, Jesus displayed liberal attitudes towards women and, in general, treated women along with other oppressed and marginal people with respect. However, Jesus' feminism when understood as deliberate opposition to patriarchal gender organization, becomes apparent only when sexism in Israel is amplified and dramatized. Some descriptions of Jewish life in the land of Israel exaggerate and overemphasize the strict separation of the sexes, the social and legal inequality of women and their exclusion from social, religious and public life. Jesus appears to support Christian women's leadership roles (Mk 16:1-10), oppose sexual double standards and marital abuse (Mk 10:2-10) and establish an inclusive and egalitarian religious community in contrast to Jewish standards and values.[3] Jesus' beliefs and actions are designated as

---

[2] For this argument, see Ringe 1985:70; Russell 1974: 87; Swidler 1979:187, 189, 194, 196; Pagels 1979:73; Ruether 1975:64; Wolff 1979:86,87; Weems 1988:87; Gray 1994:28. Non-feminist precursors include Leipoldt 1955:117-147, 1962; Jeremias 1962:396; Oepke 1957:785, 786.

[3] Carroll maintains, "so changed was Jesus' attitudes towards women from what was approved for Jews, that Christian practice unlike the Jewish law which allowed God's Covenant to be represented only in the male through circumcision, admitted woman as her own person to baptism" (1982:68; cf. Gerber 1987:90; Laurentin 1982:81). Interestingly, though, women converts to Judaism were baptized at the time of Jesus (Goldblatt 1975:68-85; Brooten 1982a:141-149; Strack and Billerbeck 1926:102-112).

un-Jewish. His feminism is not seen as a result of his Jewishness but rather as a consequence of his disassociation and alienation from Judaism.

For example, the observation that women were the first witnesses to the resurrection is highlighted "in spite of the disbelief of the `twelve,' and a lack of legal qualification as witnesses" (Russell 1974:87). Schüssler Fiorenza notes that "this fact could not have been imagined in Judaism or invented by the primitive church" (1979a:90).[4] Although law profoundly affects daily life, legal qualification for witnessing in a court of law is not needed for the kind of testimony reported in the New Testament. Moreover, in many Mediterranean cultures women play important roles in funeral customs. The presence of women during Jesus' execution and burial may be a reflection of such funeral customs. Furthermore, Jewish law allowed the testimony of women if they witnessed a death. In order to soften the scandalous fate of *agunoth* (women barred from remarriage because their husbands died or disappeared without witnesses) "the testimony of women, minors and non-Jews was permitted in a court of law" (Biale 1984:104-108; Strack and Billerbeck 1926:560). In light of this, Jesus' female disciples' testimony is well within the parameters of Jewish (patriarchal) law and need not be understood as its repudiation.

A second example concerns Jesus' prohibition of divorce as stated in Mk 10:2-10. The total prohibition of divorce is certainly not a feminist position, but if juxtaposed to a gloomy Jewish background it emerges as a liberating proposition:

> Even Jesus' pronouncements on divorce must seen in the context of a society where a woman, who had no means of support, could be cast out by her husband on the slightest pretext. The stricter attitude toward divorce in Jesus' time had the purpose of providing women with greater respect and security in marriage (Matt. 19:3-9; Mark 10:2-10; Luke 6:18) (Ruether 1975:64).[5]

Some of the texts used to substantiate the laxity of rabbinic law are found in the Mishnah (M. Gittin 9,10): R. Akiba is recorded as saying

---

[4] For similar arguments cf. Mulack 1983:274; Ruether 1975:65; Swidler 1979:100, 102, 189; Moltmann-Wendel 1980:119; Gössmann 1983:50.

[5] This argument is mostly used by non-feminists such as Leipoldt 1955:135; Oepke 1957:783; 1985:135; but also Swidler 1979:138, 174, 181, 231, 259, 326; de Croy 1982:85, 87, 74; Stagg and Stagg 1978:129, 131-135, 211.

that a man may divorce his wife if he finds another more beautiful woman, while the Hillelite school contends that a woman may be divorced if she spoils the food. Although most scholars concede that divorces were extremely rare, the reference to the rabbinic lack of restraint is used to prove Jesus' concern for women's well-being. A variation of this theme is found in Evelyn and Frank Stagg's argument that Jesus opposed the double standard of his time:

> Jesus has gone beyond Jewish perspective and practice and looked upon the wife as upon the husband, both under the same restrictions and under the same judgment in the event of divorce and remarriage. . . . Whatever the harshness here, at least there is no double standard for husbands and wives (1978:135).

The "harshness" of an uncompromising prohibition of divorce is softened by comparing it with an allegedly worse Jewish situation. Bernadette Brooten, who has consistently resisted antithetical reconstructions, interprets the statement "if she divorces her husband and marries another she commits adultery" (Mk 10:12) as a clue that Jewish women could file for divorce at the time of Jesus. Based on additional evidence from 1 Cor 7:10-11, Elephantine, Josephus and the Palestinian Talmud, Brooten concludes that women did, in fact, have the right to divorce their husbands (1982b:66-80). She maintains that Jewish women had more rights than acknowledged by Christian exegetes who depend on the negative Jewish background to redeem early Christianity.

Ironically, by reading the Gospels as evidence for and a reflection of Jewish culture in the first century, one notices that they tell a different story about women's lives: women move freely in the streets (feeding scenes, Mt 14:13; healing of the hemorrhaging woman, Lk 4:31-39), are present and visible in synagogues and the temple (healing in a synagogue, Lk 13:16; the poor widow in the temple, Mk 12:41), engage in public conversations (Canaanite woman, Mt 15:21-28; Samaritan woman, Jn 4:7-26), visit other houses and receive visitors (Mary and Martha, Lk 10:38-42; the prostitute in the house of Simon the Pharisee, Lk 7:36-50) and follow Jesus (Lk 8:3). Jesus' attitudes and behaviors are themselves evidence for liberal Jewish gender convention before the destruction of the Temple. Furthermore, most controversies in the New Testament do not focus on women but on issues such as breaking the Sabbath, associating with outcasts, sinners, lepers and prostitutes, healing, raising from the dead and forgiving sins. The opponents of Jesus do not focus on his alleged transgressions against sexual norms. Could it be that his attitudes were not that strikingly different from those of his adversaries? The relative silence of Jesus' opponents may mean that he was much less revolutionary in regard to women than generally assumed and that his teachings and social interactions with women remained, on the whole, within the scope of the acceptable. In any case, whether one evaluates his attitude towards women as moderate or progressive it should be appreciated as a Jewish attitude. Clearly, the rule of formation of antithesis is operating when restrictive customs, laws and behaviors are coded as Jewish while liberal actions and teachings are viewed as un-Jewish and anti-Jewish.

THE JEWISHNESS OF PAUL

While Jesus' attitudes towards women are portrayed as un-Jewish, readers are reminded repeatedly and ever so subtly that Paul was brought up as a Jew, trained by Pharisees and ordained as a rabbi and that he participated in his Jewish culture. In some portrayals Paul seems to suffer from a split personality. He is depicted as a person who is divided between a "Jewish" and a "Christian" self. This dilemma is most succinctly formulated by Paul Jewett:

> The apostle Paul was the heir of this contrast between the old and the new. To understand his thought about the relation of the woman to the man, one must understand that he was both a Jew and a Christian. He was a rabbi of impeccable erudition who had become an ardent disciple of Jesus Christ. And his thinking about women . . . reflects both his Jewish and his Christian experience. The traditional teaching of Judaism and the revolutionary new approach implied in the life and teaching of Jesus contributed . . . to the apostle's thinking about the relationship of the sexes. So far as he thought in terms of his Jewish background, he thought of woman as subordinate to the man for whose sake she was created (1 Cor. 11:9). But so far as he thought in terms of the new insight he had gained through the revelation of God in Christ, he thought of the woman as equal to the man in all things, the two having been made one in Christ, in whom there is neither male nor female (Gal. 3:28).
> Because these two perspectives--the Jewish and the Christian--are incompatible, there is no satisfying way to harmonize the Pauline argument for female subordination with the larger Christian vision of which the great apostle to the Gentiles was himself the great architect (1975:112-113).

Jewett resolves the tensions or contradictions in Paul's attitude towards women by identifying Judaism with sexism and Christianity with feminism.[6] By describing Paul as both a Jew and a Christian, he projects sexism onto Judaism and purifies the Christian message. Jewett invalidates and discounts Paul's authority on issues of sexual ethics by coding his prescriptions "Jewish." He uses anti-Judaism strategically to offset sexism in the Christian scriptures and presupposes that thoughts, customs and beliefs which are termed Jewish hold no legitimacy and authority for contemporary Christians. Jewett bluntly uses an antithesis between "sexist" Judaism and "feminist" Christianity.

Often, this anti-Jewish structure is activated by a discreet reminder of Paul's pharisaic training and his former love for the law.[7] Consider another, though less explicit, example of the same basic argument. In discussing Paul's alleged prescription of silence to the women of Corinth (1 Cor 14:34), Constance Parvey distinguishes between Paul's egalitarian theological thinking and "the cultural, social level, [where he] clearly identifies himself as a first century Jewish teacher" who argues "from custom," "appeals to the Torah, arguing according to the law" and uses "typical Talmudic illustration[s]" (1974:129). The troubling passage which decrees women's silence and subordination under their husbands is discounted by referring to it as a Jewish custom. The argument implies that the Paul who uses "Talmudic illustrations" (the Talmud was not codified until the fifth century C.E.) should be considered less authoritative than Paul the (egalitarian) theological thinker. Judaism is identified with patriarchal culture while Christianity claims an egalitarian theological vision.

---

[6] Non-feminist Oepke finds a "stronger than expected tension between a `progressive' and a `Jewish-reactionary line' in Paul" (1957:785).

[7] In a discussion of troubling passages, Heine mentions Paul's Jewish identity seven times in four pages and his rabbinic education five times (1986:106-109, 114). Gössmann explains that in order to understand Paul one has to note the "Tatsache, daß der christlich gewordene Paulus seine rabbinische Ausbildung nicht ablegen kann" (1983:51). Moltmann-Wendel introduces Pauline thought by quoting Gal 3:28 which overcame "the old Jewish division" between nations, social groups and sexes and goes on to say that "auch für den hochgelehrten Rabbinen ist das ein zentraler Punkt im Evangelium" (1977:22; cf. Jewett 1975:112-119, 142; S. Collins 1974:171; Mollenkott 1977:96; Carroll 1982:61; Sorge 1985:83; Mulack 1985:34; Stagg and Stagg 1978:178; Daly 1985a:84; Müller 1982:218).

A similar distinction between the Jewish and the Christian Paul can be found in Susanne Heine's *Frauen der frühen Christenheit*. She notes that Paul is a realist who makes moral and political decisions on the basis of concrete situations. She notes approvingly that Paul sees both marriage and celibacy as good, thus acknowledging bodily needs and the power of sexuality. Heine commends Paul's openness and pragmatism in matters of sexuality and marriage without acknowledging the pharisaic thinking behind his argumentation. On the contrary, she asserts: "It is striking that Paul had hardly any effect on subsequent history in what he said here on the question of mixed marriages, but the rabbinic `howler' [*rabbinischer Ausrutscher*] of 1 Cor. 11 is on everyone's lips" (1986:114). The "rabbinic howler" to which Heine refers advocates women's subordination under the head of her husband who, in turn, is under Christ who is under the Godhead. This christological hierarchy hardly originates in rabbinic thought. What seems to make it "Jewish" is its sexism. By projecting it onto Judaism the sexist affront can be removed from Christianity.[8]

The criteria for distinguishing Jewish from Christian attitudes towards women are based on their conformity to the authors' beliefs not historical considerations. One should remember that Paul, Jesus and most other protagonists in the New Testament are Jewish and argue from within a Jewish frame of reference, presupposing Jewish customs, scripture, language and law. While Paul enjoyed a pharisaic education, Jesus was called rabbi repeatedly. There is no inherent reason to assume that Jesus' thinking was not influenced by pharisaic thought. The decision to draw attention to the Jewish roots of regulations which silence women in church, require head covering and subordination while, at the same time, the Jewishness of communal breaking of bread, baptism or outreach to the marginalized are omitted, distorts the representation of Judaism. Judaism becomes the antithesis of Christianity because the Jewish origin of repressive laws and attitudes in the New Testament is emphasized while egalitarian and liberationist positions are descibed as disjunctive from Judaism. Judaism becomes antithetical to feminism, emerging as defective and

---

[8] A conservative version of this argument reads: "St. Paul's interpretation of the symbolism of this veil will perhaps be too radically Jewish, but it is nevertheless very expressive of the mentality of ancient Israel: `Christ is the head of every man, man is the head of woman. . .'" (Maertens 1969:35). Even Schüssler Fiorenza refers to Paul's christological hierarchy of God-over-Christ-over-Man-over-Woman as rabbinic thinking (1978:160).

inferior. The "good" Jesus and Paul are claimed as Christian while the "bad" Jesus and Paul are rejected as Jewish.

THE CASE OF WOMEN'S EDUCATION

Pursuing the strategies which render Judaism antithetical to Christian feminism, I want to turn the attention to the specific issue of women's religious instruction. Some interpretations of Jesus' friendship with the sisters Mary and Martha, and his endorsement of Mary's choice to sit and listen to him rather than help her sister in the kitchen, trade on an antithetical opposition between Jesus and Rabbi Eliezer ben Hyrcanus who forbade women to study Torah. Jesus' approval of women's education ("Mary has chosen the good portion, which shall not be taken from her" [Lk 10:42]) is juxtaposed to R. Eliezer's statement, "If any man gives his daughter a knowledge of the Law it is as though he taught her lechery" [*tiflut*] (M. Sotah 3:4).[9] By comparing this liberal New Testament passage with misogynist Mishnaic statements some authors argue that Jesus' attitude towards women's rights was feminist because he opposed and overcame the sexist limitations of Judaism.[10] German feminist Moltmann-Wendel remarks:

> How naturally Jesus enters the houses of women (Lk 10:38), and how equally naturally women break with tradition by behaving as disciples. Even serving at the table is impossible among strict Jews. Occasionally, however, there is a serving woman at the feet of a rabbi. But "a female disciple, who only listens to the words of the master is uncommon"--according to the Jewish philosopher Ben Chorin. "May the words of the Torah be burned but one shall not give them into the hands of women," goes the saying in late Judaism (1977:13).

R. Eliezer's words are used to create the impression of a general Jewish prohibition against women's education in religious matters in

---

[9] *The Mishnah*. Translated from the Hebrew with Introduction and Brief Explanatory Notes by Herbert Danby. Oxford: Oxford University Press. 1989.

[10] Cf. Ruether 1975:66, 1983:6; de Croy 1982:86; S. Collins 1974:175; Parvey 1974:141; Weems 1988:44-46; Swidler 1979:192; Jewett 1975:99; Moltmann-Wendel 1980:125; Mulack 1983:164, 299; Wolff 1979:83-88; Stagg and Stagg 1978:118,141; Leipoldt 1955:80ff, 124-125; Oepke 1957:784.

"late Judaism," thus implying that Jesus deliberately broke a convention when he encouraged Mary's interest in theology.

It is important to examine the source of R. Eliezer's statements and their usefulness in reconstructing Jewish social and religious life in the first century C.E. They are part of the Mishnah, a legal code redacted around 200 C.E., which, together with additional commentaries called *Gemarah*, were compiled in the Babylonian Talmud (ca. 500 C.E.) and Palestinian Talmud (ca. 450 C.E.). Although the Mishnah claims to faithfully record the opinions of first century rabbis, there is some doubt that the rabbinic system of thought was produced before the watershed events of 70 C.E. and 132-135 C.E. (Neusner 1971). The destruction of the Temple and the two Roman-Jewish wars resulted in the loss of political power in the land of Israel and were experienced as theological and political catastrophes. Rabbinic thinking was able to fill the void created by the loss of the central institutions of Temple, land and priesthood. Neusner describes the Mishnah as "a document of imagination and fantasy. It describes how things `are,' based on shreds and remnants of reality. But in large measure, it builds a social system on beams of hope" (1989:22). Furthermore, the Mishnah (just as the New Testament, for that matter) has pseudepigraphic tendencies and is not interested in historical accuracy. Instead, the rabbis intended to rewrite the past and legitimize their vision of a new and ideal order. In general, Mishnaic sayings should be used with great caution as evidence of Jewish life at the time of Jesus. The Mishnah's *Sitz im Leben* as a visionary document forbids its use as a source book of historically reliable information.

The historical, social and political contexts in which the Mishnah and later the Babylonian and Palestinian Talmuds were redacted should be compared to the environment which gave rise to the church fathers' increasing sexual and social conservatism (Plaskow 1979:9-11). In all likelihood, the rabbinic attitudes towards women, which favored the inclusion of R. Eliezer's misogynist comments were shaped by social, political and theological forces similar to those responsible for the deepening misogyny of the church fathers and their increasing verbal and legal attack on women. As Daniel Boyarin points out, the rabbis' views on women's education were not uniform but shaped by "cultural difference between Palestine and Babylonia" (1993:170). The cultural and historical contexts of the New Testament, the Mishnah, the Babylonian and Palestinian Talmuds and patristic writings must be assessed before any comparisons can be made.

R. Eliezer's statements must be understood within the context of rabbinic culture. There are no explicit *halakhic* (i.e. legal) injunctions against women's religious instruction, although there are various reasons why women are exempted from the study of Torah (Biale 1984:10-44). Wegner concludes, "As Israelites, women theoretically must study Torah (since this is not a time-contingent precept). Yet the assumption that women as a gender should not engage in study leads first to their exemption and then, inexorably, to their exclusion" (1988:162). This exemption/exclusion of women from religious instruction has become normative in patriarchal Judaism.

However, at Eliezer's time, there were voices opposing the exclusion of women. The first of Eliezer's statements occurs in the context of a discussion of *Sotah*, the ritual of the drinking of bitter water in order to determine a woman's guilt of adultery. The debate between the rabbis is whether a merit, such as study of Torah, can suspend the effects of the ordeal for a period of time.

> Hence Ben Azzai says: A man ought to give his daughter a knowledge of the Law so that if she must drink [the bitter water] she may know that the merit [that she had acquired] will hold her punishment in suspense. R. Eliezer says: If any man gives his daughter a knowledge of the Law it is as though he taught her lechery (M. Sotah 3:4).

While R. Eliezer's statement is fairly familiar to readers of Christian theology, the remark by R. Azzai is virtually unknown. Equally unknown is another Mishnaic passage which declares it a religious duty to educate sons and daughters (M. Nedarim 4:3); or the explicit permission to study religious texts given to menstruating women in the Tosefta, a supplementary collection of ritual law compiled in Palestine some time after the Mishnah in the third century C.E.:

> *Zabim* [someone with non-seminal genital emission] and *Zabot* [someone with non-menstrual bleeding], and menstruating women, and women after childbirth are permitted to read [aloud] from the Torah, the Prophets and the Writings and to study Mishnah, midrash, halakhot and aggadot, but those who have had a seminal discharge are forbidden [to engage] in all [of the aforementioned activities] (Tosefta Berakhot 2:12).[11]

---

[11] *The Tosefta*. Edited by Jacob Neusner and Richard Sarason. Translated by Tzvee Zahavy. Hoboken, NJ: Ktav Books, 1986.

If "impure" women are permitted to study and recite not only the written but also the oral Torah, how much more so women who were not menstruating? Boyarin explains the apparent discrepancies with reference to the cultural differences between Palestine and Babylonia:

> In this case, the Tosefta and Palestinian Talmud, by telling us that menstruants and parturients may study Torah, presuppose that women study and provide striking evidence for the plausibility of at least occasional study of Torah for women in that time and place. In the Babylonian Talmud, on the other hand, any voice dissenting from the stricture on the study of Torah for women was simply interpreted (in this case edited) out of existence (1993:181).

Jesus' behavior emerges as part of a Palestinian culture which apparently was more liberal with respect to gender relations than surrounding cultures. The erasure of these more liberal, "counter-hegemonic voice[s]" (Boyarin 1993:183) which approve of Jewish women's religious instruction facilitates the portrayal of Judaism as inferior to Christianity with respect to women's equality.

It is apparent that some Christian feminist authors ignore the existence of more favorable rabbinic texts, disregard the context and distort the meaning of rabbinic statements. They do so in order to present Jesus as a supporter of women's rights in contrast to "a typical Jewish setting of that time [where] women would not have been allowed to sit at the feet of a rabbi. With a few rare exceptions of rabbis' daughters, it was not considered worth while to waste time educating young women" (Parvey 1974:141). The comparison of Jesus with Eliezer is skewed and one-sided. It contrasts different categories of texts in order to render Judaism the negative foil of Christianity.

THE PRO-GENTILE BIAS

The flip side of the anti-Jewish bias is the tendency to favor Greco-Roman Gentile culture. The pro-Gentile bias is evident in the presupposition that egalitarian and feminist customs and beliefs found in the New Testament originated in Greco-Roman Gentile culture rather than the Jewish tradition. This argument has been advanced by non-feminist scholars such as Oepke who formulates this bias as a hermeneutical principle: "In general, the rule for the position of woman is: the further West, the freer" (1957:777).[12] As an "Oriental" religion, Judaism appears strange, backward and Other, and the position of women reflects an unenlightened and uncivilized condition. The early church's inclusive position on religious instruction of women is credited and attributed to a Greco-Roman Gentile women's movement.[13]

Swidler, for instance, is struck by 1 Cor 14:33-35 which specifies that women should ask their husbands for instructions at home as "a puzzling attitude in a Hellenistic world where there were so many women readers and writers; perhaps the author thought of the women as all converts from Judaism, where women for the most part were kept illiterate" (1979:337). This reductionist focus on religious difference blurs distinctions of class, race, marital status and urban versus rural living conditions which are all determinants of a woman's (or man's) level of education. To be sure, most Hellenistic women, especially enslaved, poor and women with children, were "kept illiterate." Meeks approximates that "literacy in the empire, by very rough estimate, did not exceed ten percent on average" (1986:62). This rate was certainly lower for women. At the same time, there is no reason to assume that middle and upper class Jewish women in urban centers did not know how to read and write (Kraemer 1988:77-95, n.5), particularly if Meeks is right that Jews formed "a special case among the ethnic groups with strong traditions, not least in their relatively high level of literacy" (1986:64).

The distinction between Judaism and Hellenism is not clear cut. About 10% of the Roman Empire was Jewish, an influential, well-to-do and integrated community (Isaac 1964:40-70), living in a variety of cultural environments. Kraemer has shown that women's lives varied considerably depending on their cultural and religious environment (1983, 1985a, 1985b, 1988). There was considerable economic, social and religious interaction between Gentile and Jewish women (Kraemer 1988:86-87, 90, 93). Gentile women converted to Judaism (Kraemer 1988:257-263, 289-288; Brooten 1982a:144-147) and/or were affiliated with the synagogue as "God-fearers,"

[12] This is echoed by Swidler 1979:20; Jeremias 1962:395; Leipoldt 1955:72, 80, 92, 94; and the Vatican 1977:41. For a critique of these Eurocentric and racist modern reconstructions of ancient Greece, see Bernal 1987, 1991.

[13] See S. Collins 1974:77; Pagels 1979:76; Parvey 1974:138; Swidler 1979:132-134; Raming 1982:13; Moltmann-Wendel 1980:31, 126; 1977:18-21.

unconverted believers in the God of Israel (Kraemer 1988:289). Jews were actively proselytizing among Gentiles and, apparently, especially successful among Gentile women (Balch 1981:65-80; Kraemer 1988:257-263).[14] It is unlikely that Judaism would have appealed to Greco-Roman Gentile women, if the portrayal of Jewish women as backward, illiterate and oppressed were accurate.

The pro-Gentile bias overlooks the fact that Greco-Roman philosophical and political theory espoused male supremacy as well as class and ethnic oppression. Greco-Roman Gentile women were tightly restricted by legal provisions which regulated their marital, economic and social lives. But upper and middle class women found ways of circumventing the letter of the law and gained economic power as well as some legal freedom during the first century B.C.E. and the first century C.E. (Pomeroy 1975:120-205). There is evidence that women owned property and slaves, chose and divorced their husbands and enjoyed some political influence and visibility in the public realm (Balch 1981:139-143). Nevertheless, David Balch has argued convincingly that the impact of Greco-Roman culture on Judaism and Christianity resulted in an intensification rather than a relaxation of patriarchal restrictions on Jewish and Christian women. In *Let Wives Be Submissive*, he maintains that the household codes of the New Testament accentuate the subjugation of women for apologetic reasons (1981:81-117). The subordination of women, children and slaves was stressed as an appeasement of the Roman authorities who feared that foreign cults including Dionysus, Isis, Judaism and Christianity "produced immorality (especially among Roman women) and sedition. . . . Whenever Judaism or Christianity made proselytes and changed the new convert's religious habits, they were accused of corrupting and reversing Roman social and household customs. These religious conversions were the source of the slanders about the insubordination of Christian slaves and wives" (Balch 1981:74, 119). As a response to these Roman accusations, Judaism and Christianity underscored their repressive social codes. The Jewish and Christian leadership highlighted their support of "law and order" and, in particular, of women's subordination in order to placate Roman criticism and gain political acceptance (Fiorenza 1984:71-92). The church's acculturation into the

---

[14] Acts mentions some God-fearing women who refuse to convert to Christianity (5:14; 8:3; 22:4-5) and oppose Paul (13:50; 16:14). Some converted to Christianity (17:4; 17:12).

Roman Empire did not relax gender relations but helped tighten restrictions placed on women (Schottroff 1980:104-107).

Similar modern assumptions of Gentile Hellenistic superiority can be found in some interpretations of Gal 3:28, a text which proclaims the end of social divisions between Jew and Greek, slave and free and male and female "in Christ." Some scholars maintain that this baptismal formula was composed in direct contrast to a particular Jewish prayer. The envisioned unity of Jew and Greek, slave and free, male and female is said to stand in "explicit rejection of the threefold rabbinic prayer . . . thanking God for not having made the man praying a gentile, a woman, or a slave" (Swidler 1979:322).[15] This morning prayer from the Tosefta (Jeremias 1966:31, n.66) is still used in the orthodox Jewish community.

The contrast between an ostensibly liberationist formula from the New Testament versus an oppressive Jewish prayer conforms to the rule of formation of antithesis. It denies the possibility that the Christian vision of egalitarianism and liberation has its roots in Judaism, leaving the impression that Judaism stands for racism, sexism, classism and Christianity for egalitarianism and inclusiveness. This antithesis overlooks the pervasive presence of misogynist statements in the Greco-Roman world as, for instance, the "three reasons for gratitude" variously attributed to Thales or Plato, "that I was born a human being and not a beast, next, a man and not a woman, thirdly, a Greek and not a barbarian," a rhetorical commonplace in the Hellenistic world (Meeks 1974:167; Fischel 1969:74; Thyen 1979:143).[16] One could argue that the early Christian vision of Gal 3:28 was rooted in biblical and contemporaneous Jewish culture and formulated in opposition to the moral and cultural values of the Gentile Greco-Roman world. Other Midrashic commentaries mention Israelites, Gentiles, women and slaves indiscrimnately, "I call on heaven and earth to witness that whether Gentile or Israelite, man or

[15] Cf. Heine 1986:94; Moltmann-Wendel 1977:22; Fiorenza 1978:158 (since revised to include Hellenism 1979a:88-80; 1979b:31-32; 1980:82); Ruether 1983:4.

[16] Leipoldt indignantly rejects the suggestion that the orthodox morning prayer could have parallels in the Greek world: "Man kann, wenn man die letzten Winkel der griechischen Welt auskehrt, manches Sprüchlein finden, das wir so oder so ähnlich auch bei den Juden hören. Aber ein Vergleich hat nur Sinn, wenn man gerecht abwägt" (1955:99).

woman, slave or handmaid reads this verse . . . remembers the binding of Isaac" (quoted in Gager 1985:227; cf. Strack and Billerbeck 1926:563). Although this particular Midrashic saying has been dated no earlier than the second half of the fifth century and as late as the ninth century it may oppose similar Greco-Roman literary motifs. The existence of such sayings prohibits the simple opposition between Gal 3:28 and the threefold Jewish morning prayer. The argument that Gal 3:28 was "directed against the ideal of the free Jewish male which dominated the synagogue" (Thyen 1979:139) renders Judaism the antithesis of Christian feminist values and consciously or unconsciously neglects egalitarian religious features in Judaism.

Kraemer points out another instance of a pro-Gentile bias that attributes egalitarianism to Gentile rather than Jewish societies. In *In Memory of Her*, Schüssler Fiorenza is generally cautious to avoid using Judaism as a negative backdrop, but Kraemer criticizes her thesis that the egalitarian house church was modeled after the Gentile rather than Jewish milieu:

> She [Fiorenza] contends this must have been derived from Greco-Roman religious associations, which she considers to have been inherently egalitarian. But in fact, if some Jewish synagogues accommodated the leadership and active participation of women, then her argument becomes less convincing: it might also appropriate the organizational model of the house-synagogue. In particular, Schüssler Fiorenza seems to disregard the evidence she knows for house-synagogues as early as the first century CE. (Kraemer 1985c:8).

There is no apparent historical reason to credit Greco-Palestinians with importing the model of an egalitarian house church. This pro-Gentile bias gives the impression that the Christian vision of egalitarianism was influenced by Greco-Roman values. However, it is historically flawed to assume that Greco-Roman society was more interested in egalitarianism than Jewish society. We know that most Greek philosophers and Roman politicians favored the subordination of women, slaves, and children as a *conditio sine qua non* for the proper functioning of the state (Balch 1981:1-33). Greek philosophy and political theory were based on gender, class and race stratifications (Lerner 1986:199-211; Elshtain 1981:19-55; Pomeroy 1975). It is, therefore, equally plausible to assume that the early Christian promise of an end to social distinctions is rooted in biblical Jewish ideals and juxtaposed to the Greco-Roman socio-political reality.

This chapter has delineated the mechanisms which render Judaism the antithesis of feminist reconstructions of early Christianity. By equating the (Jewish) foes of Jesus with the (patriarchal) enemies of feminism, some scholars arrive at the conclusion that Christianity and feminism are fighting the same battle. Sexism in Christianity is belittled by coding it as a Jewish attitude because texts or customs identified as Jewish lose authority and prestige. Consciously or unconsciously, Christian anti-Judaism is exploited in an attempt to undermine sexism within the church and to advance egalitarian and feminist values in Christian theology. By default, Christian antagonist attitudes towards Judaism are reinforced.

Chapter IV

JUDAISM

AS ANTITHESIS OF FEMINIST GOD-TALK

While the previous chapter looked at antithetical descriptions of Judaism in feminist exegetical appraisals of the New Testament, this chapter will document the rule of formation of antithesis in systematic theological writings. Similar mechanisms which slanted historical reconstructions of early Christianity distort some feminist revisions of theology and christology. I will look at four instances where Jesus' theological vision is reclaimed as feminist by projecting patriarchal features onto Judaism. I will also look at a womanist rereading of Hagar in which Hebrew religion symbolizes white Christianity's approval of slavery. In each case, Jewish concepts of God are cast as the enemy of liberation. While Christian theology is redeemed and invested with positive values, Jewish theology is limited to the underside of the writers' theological positions.

ABBA VERSUS THE PATRIARCHAL AUTOCRAT

For some Christians feminists, *Abba*--the Aramaic word Jesus used to address God as father--has become a jumping-off place to repudiate "the stern, judgmental autocrat of the patriarchal Jewish family" (McFague 1982:171). Jeremias has argued that *Abba* is an Aramaic term uniquely employed by Jesus in order to address God as his father. *Abba*, Jeremias proposes, should be translated as "daddy" and understood as an indication of Jesus' unique and close relationship to God. He juxtaposes Jesus' "daddy" with the legalistic, authoritarian Father God supposedly worshipped by Jesus' fellow Jews (1965:7-31; 1966). Jeremias acknowledged later that his claim could not be substantiated historically. *Abba* was not a unique term. Indeed, it seems to have been the only Aramaic term which adult Jews used to

refer either to their own father or to God. The term is documented in
pharisaic-rabbinic prayers as well as in *Targumim*, Aramaic commentaries on the Bible written at the time of Jesus (Barr 1988:28-47;
Flusser 1969:145, n.159; Finkelstein 1972:259ff; Vermes 1983:40-42).

Jeremias' retraction did not diminish the popularity of the
argument that Jesus addressed his father as *Abba* in direct rejection of
Jewish notions of authoritarian fatherhood. For Moltmann-Wendel,
Jesus' *Abba* is "an affront to any patriarchal structure. It shows no
respect and makes God familiar and near" (1986:100). Similarly, other
feminists assert that Jesus' father is intrinsically different from Jewish
beliefs about God (Mulack 1983:123,143; 1985:98,101; Ruether
1983:64-66; Carmody 1982:48: Heine 1987:18).[1]

It is certainly significant that the metaphor of the fatherhood of
God appears 170 times in the New Testament while it is mentioned
only fourteen times in the Hebrew Bible (Guist 1981:50). Yet this
startling increase in father language occurs more likely as a result of
Greco-Roman influences and not in response to Jewish patriarchy. The
frequent use in the New Testament might be an indication of the high
esteem in which Roman fathers were held. The Roman *pater familias*
held all authority and power over women, children and slaves. He
controlled the life and death of his family members. The absolute
power of the Roman father may have appealed to early Christians who
found themselves in a powerless and marginal situation. Marginalized
people may yearn for a powerful God-figure, a phenomenon which
Linda Mercandante observed in modern times with respect to the
Black church tradition:

> It is a distinct advantage for a group with little power in society to
> know that a powerful God is on its side. In this context, divine
> sovereignty means that God is ultimately and consummately in
> control, appearances often to the contrary. . . . The transcendence
> and independence of God means that no matter how powerful the
> forces of evil, no matter how hopeless-looking the situation, God

---

[1] Among feminist scholars highlighting Jesus' use of *Abba* one finds a wide
spectrum in their opposition to Judaism: On the one hand, German feminist Sorge
claims that Jesus' *Abba* "is incompatible with the nationalist, chauvinist God
imagery of the Old Testament." She calls for a "complete rejection of patriarchy
and the Old Testament," treating patriarchy and the "Old Testament" synony-
mously (1985:27,42ff,93). On the other hand, Carter Heyward mentions *Abba* to
argue for God's immanent and relational features but emphasizes that "Jesus was
not unique in and of himself" (1982:199). Yet, in mentioning *Abba* as "Jesus'
`daddy'" *(1982:11, 1989:21)* she taps into the familiar anti-Jewish argument.

has the latitude to maneuver and is free enough to clearly perceive and work out the ultimate plan (1988:97).

The Christian term *Abba* might represent an appropriation of the powerful attributes and respect owed to the Roman father rather than a repudiation of the "stern, judgmental autocrat" of the Jewish family. The feminist appropriation of the *Abba* argument revives the traditional antithesis of the judgmental God of the Old Testament versus the loving God in the New Testament.

Needless to say, the Jewish fathergod has intimate, loving, immanent and democratic features as well. A rabbinic story illustrates this notion. In a dispute between well-known rabbi Eliezer and other sages over the purity of a tile oven, Eliezer brought forward all kinds of arguments without being persuasive. So he called on a nearby carob tree to move in order to prove that he was right. The carob tree moved but the other sages were not convinced. Then Eliezer called on a stream of water to move backwards. The river reversed its course but the other scholars still were not convinced. Then he called on the walls of the house to incline. The walls threatened to collapse but the other sages still did not accept his opinion. Finally, Eliezer called on God. A Heavenly Voice (*Bat Kol*) was heard endorsing Eliezer's position.

> But R. Joshua arose and exclaimed: *"It is not in heaven.* What did he mean by this?"--Said R. Jeremiah:"That the Torah had already been given at Mount Sinai; we pay no attention to a Heavenly Voice, because Thou hast long since written in the Torah at Mount Sinai. *After the majority must one incline.* R. Nathan met Elijah and asked him: "What did the Holy One, Blessed be He, do in that hour?--He laughed [with joy], he replied, saying, `My sons have defeated Me, My sons have defeated Me' (Baba Mezia 59a-59b).[2]

The father image in this text might resemble what authors who point to Jesus' use of *Abba* have in mind: a father who encourages growth and concedes defeat in order to enable independent decision making on the part of his children. The rabbinic text is remarkable because it authorizes human independence with respect to *Halakhah*. It pictures God as one who likes being challenged and does not mind being contradicted. It hands divine endorsement to a democratic

---

[2] *The Hebrew-English Edition of the Babylonian Talmud.* Edited by I. Epstein. Translated by Salis Daiches and H. Freedman, London: Soncino Press, 1986.

concept of authority: God's interference and authority are bound by rules he himself set down in the Torah.

The rule of formation of antithesis conceals these and other anti-authoritarian Jewish texts, highlighting instead hierarchical, domineering, patriarchal images of God. Oppressive experiences, which many white Christians connect with the divine Father who is cold, dictatorial, imperious and powerful, are projected onto the Jewish God. This projection ignores that the Christian experience of God as father is a culture-specific result of accumulated cultural and theological traditions which came to the fore in the 19th and 20th centuries: the Roman legal tradition of the *pater familias*; the philosophical traditions of Aristotle and Plato and their political theories of household management; the Roman pope, symbolizing the father of the church and ruler of the Christian world; the Protestant Reformers' ideal of the patriarchal Christian family, etc. All of these traditions inform the image of a "stern, judgmental autocrat of the patriarchal family" who is rightly rejected by Christian feminists. But formulating this rejection as a denunciation of Jewish fathers feeds into the rule of formation of antithesis.

RELATIONAL TRINITY VERSUS MALE MONOTHEISM

Jürgen Moltmann prepared the ground for another antithesis, namely the difference between Christian trinitarian God language, which represents relationality, and the image of a single, male Jewish God who relates only to himself. In "Der mütterliche Vater" [The Motherly Father], Moltmann argues that

> monotheism was and is the religion of the **patriarchism** just as we may suppose, pantheism ("Mother Earth") was the religion of the earlier **matriarchism**. The Christian doctrine of the Trinity, with its affirmations about the motherly Father, represents a first step towards limiting the use of masculine terminology to express the idea of God, without, however, changing over to matriarchal conceptions (quoted in McFague 1982:173; Moltmann 1981.)

Moltmann advertises Christianity as the ideal compromise between Jewish monotheism, the religion of patriarchy, and paganism, the religion of matriarchy. Judaism, although not explicitly mentioned in the above quotation, becomes synonymous with patriarchy. Christianity "represents a first step" toward a more inclusive terminology because it supersedes the imperfect and incomplete path of (Judaism's) strict monotheism.

Moltmann argues that the Christian fathergod shows both motherly and fatherly characteristics because he gives life and begets his only son, Jesus Christ. God's suffering over Christ's crucifixion further indicates his emotional attachment and relational connection with his son, the second person of the trinity. For Moltmann, these relational, compassionate and connective features qualify trinitarian God concepts as a feminist metaphor.

Several feminist theologians have taken up Moltmann's thesis. McFague entertains the possibility of "basing feminine imagery for God on the logic of trinity" (1982:173), but she ultimately rejects the motherly father because it adds to women's invisibility and appropriates women's procreative powers. While McFague opts for the creation of new metaphors, such as "friend," in order to express the feminist experience of God more appropriately, Patricia Wilson-Kastner follows Moltmann's line of thought: "As a theological notion, the Trinity is more supportive of feminist values than is a strict monotheism. Popular monotheism is by far more of a support for patriarchy than trinitarianism, because the one God is always imagined as a male" (1983:122; cf. Brown 1987:354-357). Judaism is once more identified with patriarchy.

One could argue that strict, imageless monotheism, as promoted by Judaism and Islam, simplifies the development and application of inclusive and female God language. There is no theological argument against female God language in these traditions, which puts Jewish and Muslim women in a better theological position. The trinitarian expression of patriarchal monotheism has no advantages for feminists since the trinitarian God has usually been imagined as all-male. Mary Daly's comments may be acid but to the point. She characterizes the trinity as

> the original **Love Story**, performed by the Supreme All Male Cast. . . . It is the "sublime" (and therefore disguised) erotic male homosexual **mythos**, the perfect all-male marriage, the best boys club, the model monastery, the supreme Men's Association, the mold for all varieties of male monogender mating (1978:38).

One can argue that trinitarian God language heightens theological sexism because the Son's gender reinforces the masculinity of the Father. Judith Plaskow puts it succinctly: "After all **their** God came down to earth incarnate in human **male** form. They have worse problems than we do" (1979:17). Time and again, christology and Jesus' incarnation in human male form have been used against women. Christ's masculinity was used against women by the Vatican's declaration on the ordination of women (Vatican 1977). Jesus' masculinity became the supreme reason for women's rejection as priests because women cannot symbolize Jesus. The contrast with Jewish monotheism serves to disguise feminist conflicts with trinitarian God language, rendering it superior and redeemable. Like Virginia Woolf's magic mirror Judaism serves to reflect a more appealing and feminist Christianity.

The characterization of Judaism as male monotheism disregards feminine and relational features of Jewish God language. For instance, the "Heavenly Voice" (*Bat Kol*), mentioned in the previous section, is female. God speaks in a personified female voice. God's *Shekhinah*, God's presence on earth among the people, is female. The *Shekhinah* shares suffering and oppression with the people of Israel in exile after the destruction of the Temple. She is God's immanence who is compassionate and co-suffering with the people.

> Described as daughter, bride, mother, moon, sea, faith, wisdom, speech and a myriad of other figures, usually but not always feminine by fact or association, the *Shekhinah* is the chief object of both the divine and the human search for wholeness and perfection. She is the bride of God within God, mother of the world and feminine side of the divine self, in no way fully separable from the male self of God. Indeed the root of all evil, both cosmic and human, is the attempt to bring about such separation (Green 1983:255).

God's diverse names in the Hebrew Bible have been interpreted by the rabbis as God's different aspects and components, sometimes in conflict with each other. The rabbis used textual openings to create new metaphors such as *Hokhmah*, wisdom (Wisdom 8:3-6; 9:1-4), *Ruach*, God's spirit, or *Torah*, God's law and commandments, some of which are personified as female (cf. Swidler 1979:49-54). These metaphors enable Jews to express God's relationality, immanence and accessibility. While the Jewish tradition has maintained strict, imageless monotheism, it has also created a rich pool of metaphors for the divine. Judith Plaskow argues that one must not mistake monotheism with "monolatry," a restriction of the divine to only one image, but rather imagine God as being all-embracing (1990:151-168; cf. McFague 1982). Indeed, Plaskow's "inclusive monotheism" opens the door to the "affirmation of multiple images for God" which "reflect the multiplicity both of a pluralistic Israel and of a cosmic community" which will make "God truly . . . one--which is to say, all in all" (1990:151).

Far from being reduced to one side of various dualistic oppositions, such as justice (versus compassion), transcendence (versus immanence), Oneness (versus relationality), masculinity (versus femininity), Jewish God language offers enough resources for feminists to incorporate their insights into revisions of Judaism. The rule of formation of antithesis conceals the wealth and diversity of existing Jewish God concepts.

PATERNAL LOVE VERSUS MATERNAL LOVE

Psychology, which distinguishes between feminine and masculine modes of being, has found its way into feminist theology by way of C.G. Jung (1955), Erich Neuman (1963) and Erich Fromm (1974). The theory that there is an essential difference between maternal love (given unconditionally) and paternal love (dependent on a child's performance) was derived from Jungian psychology and applied to the cultural and theological world. Matriarchal religion, so the argument goes, was built on the feminine principle. According to Fromm, the Goddess, like nature, accepts and loves everybody simply for being born, while the patriarchal fathergod introduces ethical principles and accepts only those who comply with ethical standards and are able to please him. Feminists, such as Moltmann-Wendel, have adopted this argument:

> Since Johann Jakob Bachhofen investigated early cultures and religions in the last century and discovered in matriarchal cultures this love which gives itself unconditionally to strangers, we have learned to distinguish between matriarchal and patriarchal love. According to Erich Fromm "the essence of paternal love" consists in imposing demands, establishing laws and making love for the son dependent on his obeying orders (1986:169).

The "essence of paternal love" corresponds to Protestant descriptions of Judaism as a legalistic religion. Moltmann-Wendel uses a traditional anti-Jewish antithesis for her feminist reinterpretation of Christian theology. She argues that Jesus' love is an example of the feminine, matriarchal principle of unconditional love established over against Jewish patriarchal concepts. "For Paul, freedom from the law, from the Jewish law, was the basic experience rooted in Christ." This experience, like Luther's *sola fide*, "contains a hidden matriarchal content--despite its `manifest patriarchal character'" (1986:152).

Although Moltmann-Wendel does not elaborate further on the theme of "Jewish legalism," her argument presupposes and exploits the traditional Lutheran antithesis of law versus grace. The Christian polemic against legalism, which has been part of the Christian anti-Jewish tradition since the New Testament, is based on a false dualism of love and law. Feminists are in danger of perpetuating dualistic thinking by wedding the old opposition with a new dichotomy of maternal versus paternal, or female versus male language. For instance, Sheila Collins' use of the theory that the left hemisphere of the brain specializes in logical, rational thinking while the right side operates in more intuitive and emotional ways lends itself to classic characterizations of Judaism as legalistic and rigid while Christianity can claim the right brain, female, matriarchal tradition of intuition, spontaneity, love, spirituality and grace (1974:99, 101, 106, 170-171). Similarly, Gilligan's distinction between male and female modes of moral decision-making--where women's choices connote mutuality and concern for relation, while male morality revolves around principles of justice and ethical norms--may also potentially be applied to Christianity (grace) and Judaism (law).[3]

According to Neusner, an apologetic midrash in Leviticus Rabbah, one of the oldest Midrashim extant (5th century C.E.), addresses Christian charges of legalism:

> Said R. Simeon b. Yohai, "[The matter may be compared] to a king who has only one son. Every day he would give instructions to his steward, saying to him, `Make sure my son eats, make sure my son drinks, make sure my son goes to school, make sure my son comes home from school.' So every day the Holy One, blessed be he, gave instructions to Moses, saying, `Command the children of Israel,' `Say to the children of Israel,' `Speak to the children of Israel'" (Leviticus Rabbah II.V a-b, quoted in Neusner 1987:90).

The Jewish tradition understands God's commandments as expressions of God's concern and love, and not as their opposite. The Midrash gives a glimpse of fatherly love which seems quite "maternal," namely loving concern for a child's daily necessities. In our cultures it is

---

[3] For an excellent critique of these dualisms, see Harding 1986:163-197.

usually mothers who fuss about what children eat and drink, what they wear, when they go to school or come home. The mother's love sets rules in a household to insure everybody's well-being. Similarly, Jewish faith asserts that God sets rules for Jews, "because the Lord loves you and is keeping the oath which he swore to your fathers. . . You shall therefore be careful to do the commandments . . . which I command you this day" (Dt 7:7,11). Contrary to Christian descriptions of Jewish legalism, God's acceptance and love predates human efforts to keep the commandments. Luther's "justification by faith" is a restatement of the Hebrew Bible's understanding of election and covenant, and not a radically new affirmation of grace over against law.

It is disturbing that Moltmann-Wendel portrays Jesus as side-stepping patriarchy and appropriating matriarchal religion. The "love of God which Jesus demonstrates in actions and in narratives has clear relationships with the traditions of women" (1986:170). She purges patriarchy from the "centre of Christianity" (1986:169) and claims it as less patriarchal than Judaism.

THE ANIMA-INTEGRATED JESUS

Jung's psychological theory has influenced some feminist re-readings of the life and teaching of Jesus of Nazareth. This is especially true for three German authors, Hanna Wolff (1979, 1981), Christa Mulack (1983, 1985, 1987) and Maria Kassel (1986), who undertake a psycho-theological analysis of Jesus. All three observe that Jesus' psyche progresses toward greater psychological wholeness by increasingly integrating his anima. "Anima" is men's archetypal feminine; "animus" is women's archetypal masculine.[4] Jung proposes that the integration of one's repressed feminine or masculine side

---

[4] Jung's analysis of the Hebrew God's integration of the anima after his encounter with Job precedes these anti-Jewish assessments of Jesus (1955). For Jung, God realizes his own injustice and violence in his clash with Job. Job's innocence forces God to realize that he can be unjust and violent. God recognizes his failure to keep the covenant in which he promised to protect the righteous and innocent while punishing the unjust. Realizing this, God integrates his repressed feminine side. The elevation of Sophia (wisdom, *Hokhmah*, Mary) into heaven leads to Sacred Marriage (Hierosgamos) and subsequently to Jesus' birth. Jesus is the climax of God's union with the feminine/Goddess. Since Jews fail to acknowledge this they remain in an immature state.

which is buried in the unconscious is a prerequisite for a whole and mature self.

All three authors measure Jesus' success at anima integration by the degree of his disassociation from Judaism. They define the Jewish distinctions between pure and impure, Jewish and non-Jewish and the Sabbath and weekdays as psychologically immature and unhealthy, and equate Jesus' opposition to these distinctions with his psychological development towards wholeness.

For the non-feminist Hanna Wolff, Jesus' acceptance of his anima manifests itself when he confronts and overcomes the "four catch words: **hypocrisy, mercilessness, formalism and trade** (*Rechtshandel*)" (Wolff 1979:134). These catch words supposedly characterize Judaism at the time of Jesus (Wolff 1979:123,112; also Weiler 1984:85,334). Ritualism, merit thinking, expectation of rewards and lack of trust and love in God are Judaism's shortcomings which Jesus must overcome. Jesus' psychological growth coincides with his rejection of, and alienation from, Judaism.

The encounters of Jesus with the Samaritan woman (Jn 4:7-30) or Canaanite woman (Mt 15:20-28; Mk 7:24-30) are interpreted as turning points in Jesus' development. In both instances, the women are foreign and confront Jesus with his own Jewish sexism and racism (Kassel 1986:21-217; Mulack 1983:284-288; Wolff 1979:153; cf. Ringe 1985:68,70,71). For Mulack, Jesus' conversation with the Samaritan women reveals his *"jüdischer Nationalstolz"* and *"Judenstolz"* (Jewish national pride) (1983:289). Her choice of words implies, in a derogatory fashion, that Judaism connotes arrogance, elitism and contempt for others. When Jesus rebuts the Canaanite woman he confronts his (Jewish) shadow and realizes that the criteria for his actions must not be restricted to ethnicity and gender but must become a universal concern for weakness.

> He is not yet the savior of humanity but only the son of David whose national pride prevents him from responding to this desperate woman with even one word. This shows a typical Bina-attitude which divides, separates into Jewish-non-Jewish, pure-impure and whatever these divisions may be called. . . . Only after he recognizes his own anima as a dog is he willing to satisfy the feminine (Mulack 1983:284,286).

Mulack considers Jewish particularity to be identical with repression of the feminine and, thus, a psychologically inadequate and inferior position.[5] Similarly, Kassel describes Jewish particularity as a "religious-national shadow projection which originates in the knowledge of chosenness in the Israelite-Jewish faith" (1986:212). Kassel and Mulack equate Jewish particularism with psychological deficiency and Christian universalism with psychological maturity. By attacking the Jewish claim to be different as chauvinistic, and by equating the distinctiveness of Jews with arrogance and racism, these writers attack the very heart of Judaism.

As Catherine Keller observes, human beings need distinctions in order to relate to one another. She defends difference by pointing out that "relation does not seek sameness, for then it would not find any others with whom to relate, it would be trapped in narcissism and without interchange. Far from obliterating distinctness, the relational world view thrives on difference" (1986a:120). It is not distinction and difference feminists should oppose, Keller maintains, but rather dualistic hierarchies. Feminist values of relationality and relationship presuppose difference. A relational theology or philosophy, therefore, cherishes the Other as the one to whom one can relate.

Jewish feminists have wrestled with the question of whether the Jewish understanding of holiness as separation and distinction is theologically redeemable or whether it inevitably invites dualistic hierarchies and the creation of an Other. After all, *Kadosh*, the Hebrew word for holy, means "to be separate." The central tenants of Judaism rest on the notion of holiness as separation, such as *Kashrut*, the separation of certain foods, Shabbat, the separation between the week and the day of rest and the separation of the people of Israel as a holy nation, distinguishing between Jew and non-Jew. Drorah Setel points out that

> this separational concern does not exclusively **constitute** Judaism, even from the most traditional perspective. To begin with, there are more relational concerns tied to social justice or the more general concept of *tikkun olam*, the "repair of the world," which defines the human task as one of reunifying a fragmented creation. Underlying these and other relational concepts is the central belief in the unity of God/ess and, hence of creation (1986:116).

[5] For a detailed analysis of Mulack's anti-Judaism, see Brockmann 1987:70-93; Flatters 1988a:48, 1988b:164-181; and Mulack's response 1988:40.

While Setel mitigates the centrality of separations by pointing to the task of reunification, Judith Plaskow rejects the concept of chosenness and replaces it with "the much less dramatic `distinctiveness.' . . . The term distinctiveness suggests . . . that the relation between these various communities--Jewish to non-Jewish, Jewish to Jewish--should be understood not in terms of hierarchical differentiation but in terms of part and whole" (1990:105). In either case, Jewish feminists are unlikely to embrace the (white?) Christian vision of a universal community where all differences and separations are overcome. The Jungian-feminist equation of Jewish particularism with immaturity and Christian universalism with psychological health is a troubling continuation of the rule of formation of antithesis.[6]

THE GOD OF SLAVE-HOLDERS

The last example stands somewhat apart from the rest of this chapter. Delores Williams' *Sisters in the Wilderness* takes a narrative from the Hebrew Bible as the paradigm for womanist theology. Williams stands in the tradition of the Black church whose theology resonates with the stories of the Hebrew Bible. The Black church and Black liberation theology have traditionally understood Christian theology in light of God's promise of liberation to the Israelites in Egypt. The exodus story became the paradigm, reaffirmed in the liberating presence and activity of Jesus Christ. White Christian theology often saw the meaning of Christ in contrast to, or superseding, the events in the Hebrew Bible. The Black church, on the other hand, celebrated the heroes of the Hebrew Bible and found meaning in their struggles. "Through hearing and reading the story of the Jews, blacks were enabled to perceive the activity of God in their own community" (Hoyt 1991:30). Believers cheered Moses on in his uneven confrontation with Pharaoh, wept with Jeremiah along the rivers of Babylon and feared for Daniel in the lions's den. Black theology has understood Jesus (and its own faith) in continuity with the Hebrew tradition and, by and large, escaped the rule of formation of antithesis otherwise prominent in (Protestant) theological thinking.

[6] These Jungian approaches to Jesus' psychological development should be distinguished from Jungian religious feminists such as Wehr (1987) and Goldenberg (1979) who do not identify Judaism as psychologically immature.

Delores Williams presents the first, in-depth "Christian theology (or god-talk) from the point of view of African-American women" (1993:1). She critiques Black liberation theology whose "validating biblical paradigm in the Hebrew testament was the exodus event when God delivered the oppressed Hebrew slaves from their oppression in Egypt" as androcentric, and points instead to "the striking similarities between Hagar's story and the story of African-American women" (1993:2, 3). In Williams' womanist theology of "survival/quality of life," Hagar's predicament becomes paradigmatic for understanding African-American women's historic, social, political and religious experience. The story of Abram, Sarai and Hagar provides a powerful model to expose slavery and subsequent white-Black relations in America, as well as white women's participation in the oppression of Black women. Through the paradigm of Hagar's struggle for survival and well-being in the face of the combined forces of racism and sexism, Williams marks womanist theology's unique vantage point between white feminist theology and Black liberation theology.

The choice of Hagar as the paradigm for womanist theology is powerful and persuasive. If one is concerned about anti-Judaism, however, the theological embrace of the Egyptian slave who suffers under her Hebrew mistress leads to a troubling role reversal: the former victims, the Israelites, become slave-holders, while the former victimizers, the Egyptians, are now represented as/by a "female slave of African descent" (Williams 1993:26ff). Drawing attention to the victim of the victims, Williams challenges Cone and others who have highlighted the affinity between the African-American community's experience of "life in bondage and that of the ancient Israelites in Egypt" (1993:148):

> Have they, in the use of the Bible, identified so thoroughly with the theme of Israel's election that they have not seen the oppressed of the oppressed in scripture? Have they identified so completely with Israel's liberation that they have been blind to the awful reality of victims making victims in the Bible? (1993:149)

The Israelites are displaced as the community with whom (oppressed) African-Americans can and should identify. Instead, another group, the oppressed of the oppressed, primarily non-Hebrew, take their place (cf. Williams 1993:144-153). The traditional theological alliance between African-Americans and the Israelites of the Bible is broken up. To adopt Hagar, the Egyptian slave of the Hebrew mistress, can potentially turn the Hebrews into the antithesis of womanist theology and ethics.

While it is true that Hebrew society legally condoned slavery and allowed harsher treatment for non-Hebrew slaves, it seems dangerous to project the American experience of racially based chattel slavery onto the biblical text, and to cast Jews into the role of the (Southern, Christian) slave master and mistress. Drawing on the Afrocentric reclamation of Egypt as an African civilization (cf. Copher 1991:146-164; Bailey 1991:165-184; Bernal 1987:1-75) Williams combines Hagar's status as a slave with the Blackness of Egyptian culture to read African-American women's experience of slavery through the biblical text. This automatically identifies the Hebrews as white although there is general agreement that "the specific racial type of the biblical Hebrews is itself quite difficult to determine" (Felder 1991:128). Since the Egyptian Hagar is the powerless victim in the hands of the powerful Hebrews, the power dynamics of the Exodus narrative are reversed.

> The Abrahamic period in Israel is usually designated as lasting from 2000 to 1720 B.C.E. This is the time of Egypt's Middle Kingdom, during which period the areas of Damascus (Syria) and Canaan remained under the domination of Egypt. This is also the time of the twelfth dynasty in Egypt. Since Egypt was in a strong military position at that time, it certainly would not have allowed its citizens to be held as slaves by those who were under its domination. As a matter of fact, most of the slaves in Egypt during the Middle Kingdom were Asiatic (Waters 1991:189).

Without minimizing the horror of Hagar's story (Gen 16-23), the characterization of the Egyptians as the (Black) underdogs and of Abram and Sarai as the (white) "wealthy Hebrew slave-holding family" (Williams 1993:15) is problematic.

Although I agree with Williams that the God of Abram and Sarai is implicated in the mistreatment of Hagar, the suggestion that Hagar encountered a God other than "the God of the slave-holders Sarai and Abram and the fact that she does not name her God in accord with their [Sarai and Abram's] patriarchal traditions" (1993:25) is potentially anti-Jewish. Williams attributes Hagar's naming of God to "Egyptian tradition," thus attributing the most empowering and liberating moment in the Hagar narrative to her Egyptian identity. When Williams asks whether "Hagar's naming action [is] a strike against the ultimate head of this ancient Hebrew family . . . [namely] its patriarchal God" (1993:26) she comes close to suggesting that the

Hebrew God is uniquely allied with slavery and patriarchy, while Hagar's Egyptian heritage is less compromised by such oppressive practices.

This reading renounces identification with the Hebrews as victims of slavery. God's liberating promise is replaced by a God of slave-holders who approved and condoned the enslavement of non-Hebrew peoples. This reading comes at a time of tensions between the Black and Jewish communities and of an increasing acceptance of theories which blame Jews for much of the slave trade (Nation of Islam 1991; Austen 1994:65-69; cf. Martin 1993). Although Williams does not explicitly enter the debate on the Jewish role in slavery, *Sisters in the Wilderness* predisposes the readers to expect a higher involvement of Jews in the enslavement and oppression of non-Jews, supposedly endorsed and condoned by their God. This interpretation does not counteract current anti-Jewish perceptions in the Black community of Jews as wealthy and powerful agents in the slave trade.

Summing up, some feminist and womanist reformulations of God language project unwelcome features of patriarchal theology and christology onto Judaism: the Christian *Abba* provides an opportunity to repudiate the distant, authoritarian autocrat; the trinitarian concept is redeemed as relational over against a single, male God; the notion of maternal love, recalling the Lutheran doctrine of justification by faith, is contrasted with Jewish law and paternal love; the anima-integrated, psychologically mature Jesus is set over against Judaism haunted by a collective shadow of dualistic separations; the Egyptian slave Hagar renounces racism and sexism by rejecting the God of Hebrew slave-holders. In each case, anti-Judaism is adopted as a device to enhance Christian feminist and womanist theological argumentation by investing it with new values and visions.

Chapter V

JUDAISM

AS ANTITHESIS OF THE GODDESS

The rule of formation of antithesis is found in those feminist writings which incorporate models of ancient Near Eastern Goddesses and are based on the theory of matriarchal religions (Stone 1978; Ochs 1977; Ochshorn 1981; Spretnak 1978; Weiler 1984; Lerner 1986; Christ 1987). Scholars who are less dependent on historical models of the Goddess but who use ritual and literary approaches to feminist spirituality exhibit less or no anti-Jewish tendencies since they can create post-Christian or post-Jewish spirituality without recourse to Christian representations of Jewish symbolism and practice (Starhawk 1979, 1982; Christ 1980; Adler 1979; Downing 1984). Those feminist authors who argue from historical materials are at risk of depicting the status of women in Hebrew society and biblical monotheism in antithetical ways.

THE STATUS OF WOMEN IN THE HEBREW BIBLE

Beginning with the founding fathers of matriarchal scholarship, e.g. Bachofen (1967), Engels (1970), Graves (1978) and Neumann (1963), the idea of matriarchy has had utopian overtones. The discovery of cultures whose religion centered on Goddesses led 19th century evolutionary, political, psychological and literary thinkers to propose the existence of matriarchies (cf. Wacker's excellent overview 1988:204-223). Their theories about mother-worshipping cultures were based on cross-cultural comparisons of symbols and myths drawn from studies in archaeology, ethnography, ritual studies, mythology and psychology. They synthesized evidence from European fairy tales, classical Greek epics, ancient Near Eastern and Mediterranean cultures, observations of "primitive" cultures and, later, dream analysis.

These androcentric thinkers differed sharply in their evaluations of matriarchy. Some, like Bachofen, considered matriarchy an inferior stage in the development of human civilization, while Engels saw matriarchy as humanity's communist past which foreshadowed the future.

For feminist writers matriarchy represents an ideal, utopian time in history where peace and harmony reigned, and where alienation between women and men, humanity and nature and humanity and the deity did not exist. Some portrayals evoke associations with paradise. For German feminist Monheim-Geffert's matriarchy embodies the Garden of Eden: "Seen altogether the world view and life style of Goddess worshipers proves to be much more integrated, without separating the world into good and evil. It reflects the original harmony of paradise" (1982:209). In this instance, attributes and qualities are bestowed on matriarchy which render this historical time theologically, morally, politically and socially superior. These claims are difficult to substantiate historically. Oftentimes, notions of matriarchies as cultures in which peace, equality and prosperity reigned are based on leaps of faith.

The theory of matriarchy is largely based on the interpretation of symbols. Depictions of Goddesses, artifacts and symbolic representations of women's bodies often substitute for textual evidence which could attest to societies in which women enjoyed equal (if not more) social, economic, political and religious power to men (Binford 1982:541-549). Although some societies are characterized by matrilineality and matrilocality, the emotional, social and theological significance of this organization eludes the researcher. Virtually all textual information about women's status comes from patriarchal societies and attests to women's subjugation. Legal texts, economic records and historical accounts such as the Bible and the Code of Hammurabi depict patriarchal cultures in which the public realm was dominated by men.

In the absence of written records, the social position of matriarchal women is described by antithetical strategies. In *When God Was a Woman*, Merlin Stone notes that "in contrast to the economic, legal and social position of women all about them, the position of the Israelite women exhibits the effects of the almost total acceptance of the male deity Yahweh, and the patriarchal society that accompanied it" (1978:55). The assumption that the belief in the "male" deity YHWH had direct social implications (as substantiated by the low status of women in the Hebrew Bible) can then be reversed to "prove" that belief in Goddesses elevated the status of matriarchal women. Stone emphasizes the oppressed situation of Hebrew women in order to deduce a higher status of women in pagan religions. The following statement illustrates this strategy of reversal: "Just as the Hebrews prayed for sons and rejoiced when male heirs were born . . . in matrilineal societies the birth of daughters was likely to have been considered a special blessing" (1978:60). The Hebrew Bible becomes the primary example of a patriarchal society against which other societies are measured. Passages from the Hebrew Bible are taken out of context and used selectively as a backdrop to enhance the superiority of pagan religion.

The portrayal of Hebrew culture as prototype of patriarchy overlooks the fact that Israel was a small, insignificant nation surrounded and dominated by such empires as Mesopotamia, Babylonia and Egypt. Rather than being a patriarchal trend setter, Hebrew society was influenced by surrounding cultures and legal codes, such as the Mesopotamian Code of Hammurabi and Middle Assyrian law. These codes are closely related to Deuteronomic law (Lerner 1986: 76-141; Teubal 1984:3-71; Swidler 1979:13). The Code of Hammurabi, for instance, denies women the right to divorce and makes it easy for men. It holds women accountable in cases of rape and adultery and invests the father with sole familial authority. This corresponds to Israelite women's restrictions: they are placed under the authority of father, husband and brothers of husband; they are subjected to arranged marriages, polygyny, sexual double standards and are prevented from inheriting (exceptions notwithstanding). The fate of Hebrew women is hardly the result of "an isolated patriarchal society" as Stone claims (1978:54), but rather the result of larger cultural forces which determined the legal, economic and social situation of women in the Near East between 2500-1000 B.C.E., irrespective of religious and tribal-ethnic factors.

German feminist theologian Gerda Weiler argues that male supremacy and violence against women are specific characteristics of deuteronomist monotheism. Weiler claims that non-monotheistic and pre-monotheistic women enjoyed greater respect and fewer restrictions and that deuteronomist monotheism was exceptionally resolute in its patriarchal oppression:

> It was inevitable that together with the development of patriarchal religions, the position of woman in society would also be upset. . . . The victorious march of the deuteronomist *Geisteshaltung* (ideology) in Judah accomplished the radical oppression of woman.

> The scope of misogynous polemic in the Old Testament reaches
> from instructions of petty restrictions of women's rights in everyday
> life to the justification of the brutal murder of women (1984:386).

This representation is sustained by a selective emphasis on oppressive aspects of sexual relations in ancient Israel. Portrayals of Hebrew women's social lives serve to exemplify patriarchal evil and are contrasted with non-Hebrew women whose lives are assessed more sympathetically.

Historian Gerda Lerner admits that the Goddess religions of the empires surrounding Israel were patriarchal. However, in contrast to Stone and Weiler who attempt to prove polytheistic women's high social status by comparing it to Hebrew women, Lerner minimizes the significance of her observation that polytheistic women were subjugated even while the Goddess reigned high. She maintains that pagan women were better off even if their legal, economic and social standing was quite comparable to that of Hebrew women:

> No matter how degraded and commodified the reproductive and
> sexual power of women was in real life, their essential equality
> could not be banished from thought and feeling as long as the
> goddesses lived and were believed to rule human life. Women must
> have found their likeness in the goddesses, as men found theirs in
> the male gods. There was a perceived and essential equality of
> human beings before the gods, which must have radiated out into
> daily life (1986:160).

For Lerner, Goddess worship remains superior to Hebrew monotheism even when the existence of Goddesses does not entail higher social status for women. The fact that there may have been no significant differences in women's social existence--whether they lived in a monotheistic or polytheistic patriarchal culture--is ignored. Instead, Lerner postulates an "essential quality" in pagan women's experience which, in her opinion, was lacking in Hebrew monotheism.

Lerner evaluates biblical stories on the basis of their compliance with this general thesis: while she rules out the Song of Songs as historical evidence for women's social status she asserts that Lot's offering of his virgin daughter to be raped "reflects a historic social condition" (Lerner 1986:173).

> The Song of Songs is so difficult to interpret and bring into
> historical perspective that it seems unreasonable to make inferences
> from it as to the actual status of women; it needs to be treated as
> a literary creation. . . . It does not seem possible to me to use it as

the basis for generalizations about the actual conditions of women
in Hebrew society (Lerner 1986:117).

This assessment is not shared by biblical exegetes. Carol Meyers, for
example, considers it an accurate reflection of gender dynamics in the
private setting of the family (1988:177-181). Phyllis Trible interprets
the Song of Songs as a redemptive text where "there is no male
dominance, no female subordination, and no stereotyping of either sex.
Specifically, the portrayal of the woman defies the connotation of
`second sex.' She works keeping vineyards and pasturing flock.
Throughout the Song she is independent, fully the equal of the man"
(1984:161). Even Gerda Weiler accepts the Song of Songs as historically accurate, albeit for a matriarchal Israel which used it as a
cultic text during matriarchal Sacred Marriage rituals (1984:270-309).
If egalitarian texts, as in Lerner's case, are not admitted as historical
evidence, the comparison between Hebrew women's lives and those of
surrounding polytheistic cultures will unfold accordingly.

A disturbing number of authors find Hebrew religion and
society accurately symbolized in stories and legislation concerning
rape. Both Genesis 19:1-11, where Lot volunteers his virgin daughters
to be gang raped, and Judges 20, the Levite's concubine's rape and
dismemberment, are presented as common events and examples of
"normal" male-female relations (Lerner 1986:170-179; Weiler 1984:
389-390; Stone 1978:190-192; Brownmiller 1975:12). I would surmise
that these stories were told to depict exceptionally horrifying crimes
and do not describe "the social attitudes and practices of the Hebrews
at the time when the book of Judges was written and finally redacted,"
as Ochshorn maintains (1981:156). They hardly "illustrate," as Daly
claims, "the value placed upon women in the Old Testament"
(1973:117).

I certainly do not want to defend the Hebrew Bible's record on
rape. As the product of a patriarchal world, it does not perceive rape
from the perspective of the female victim. Legally, the injured party
of a rape is the husband or father, not the woman. The reader waits in
vain for God's intervention and condemnation of the crime. There is
apparently no divine support for the rejected Hagar, raped Tamar,
dismembered Levite's concubine and sacrificed Jephtah's daughter
(Trible 1984). The Hebrew God does not seem to stand at the side of
female victims. It is nevertheless questionable to characterize the
world of the Hebrew Bible as an essentially rapist culture where such
violations were common and accepted practice.

Without doubt, the legal treatment of rape in the Hebrew Bible is abhorrent to modern sensitivities. Rape in the Hebrew Bible "was seen as an offense against men, not against their female property" (Daly 1973:117); a woman who lost her virginity in the rape had to be married by the rapist who lost his right to divorce her (Dt 22:28-29). If the rape occurred outside the city, the perpetrator was stoned, while the woman went free (Dt 22:25). If a rape happened in town and the woman failed to scream, the victim was considered an adulteress and stoned together with the rapist (Dt 22:23). Although these laws are a far cry from justice, they must be compared to surrounding polytheistic (patriarchal) nations such as polytheist Assyria: the rapist also had to marry his virginal victim yet, if he was married, his wife was given "to be ravished."[1] If the rapist insisted that he had been seduced, his wife was spared and he merely paid a fine to the victim's father. Clearly, the presence of Goddesses did not protect women's sexual integrity any better than monotheism did in neighboring Israel.

What makes these portrayals of Hebrew women anti-Jewish is the conjecture that monotheistic Israel practiced patriarchal violence over and above the degradation suffered by women in neighboring polytheistic societies. Until scriptural evidence for a matriarchal society in which women enjoyed public power and religious influence is found, feminists need to be careful in using the Hebrew Bible as an antithesis of matriarchy, thereby reducing Hebrew culture and religion to a paradigm of patriarchy.

GODDESS THEALOGY

Four political movements accentuate contemporary feminist readings of the Bible and buttress antithetical oppositions: first, the peace movement which opposes war and militarism; second, liberation movements which confront hierarchical authoritarianism; third, the ecology movement which contests the image of God as transcendent and in control of nature; and fourth, the women's movement which opposes male dominated religion and male God imagery. Many white

[1] "Middle Assyrian Law." Translated by Theophile Meeks. In *Ancient Near Eastern Texts Related to the Old Testament*. Edited by James Pritchard. Princeton, NJ: Princeton University, 1969:189.

North American and Western European Christians are profoundly alienated from traditional metaphors which symbolize God as Lord, Warrior, King, transcendent Creator and Father. Alternative symbols which break the link between militarism and religion and which support democracy, egalitarianism and pluralism are sorely needed. Shifting perceptions of sexuality, the body and nature create a need to find new models for more immanent and relational expressions of the divine. Last not least, traditional God language has systematically excluded women's voices and experiences, and many women are in the process of conceiving new symbolic expressions of women's spirituality. The rule of formation of antithesis can be found in feminist reclamations of Near Eastern Goddesses which identify YHWH with militarism, despotism, alienation from nature and sexism.

YHWH as Warrior God

The depiction of YHWH as a warrior god precedes the onset of feminist writings but feminist scholars have adopted this portrayal and have highlighted YHWH's involvement in, and legitimization of, military exploits. At the same time, the significance of the observation that all ancient Near Eastern deities, male or female, supported militarism is minimized. When similar activities are evaluated and appraised differently, depending on whose military virtues are lauded, the rule of formation of antithesis is at work. It instills the subtle impression that the Hebrew God is significantly more involved in military ventures than his female Near Eastern counterparts.

Neo-pagan thealogian Carol Christ rejects the Hebrew God because he is a "Holy Warrior." She maintains that as a white North American woman actively involved in the peace movement this "God of war stands for far too much that I stand against" (1987:77). She objects to the image of a God who liberates his people militarily and leads them out of Egypt with a strong arm. The biblical God promises a land which must first be conquered and he pledges protection against enemies who later threaten the land. No doubt, the biblical God is engaged in warfare.

Yet, so were ancient Goddesses who did not love peace any more than their male counterparts. The femininity of Near Eastern Goddesses did not preclude their interest and expertise in military matters. A Mesopotamian prayer to the Goddess Ishtar lauds her military strength:

I pray to thee, O Lady of ladies . . .
O supporter of arms, who determines battle,
O possessor of all divine power, who wears the crown of dominion,
. . .
O star of lamentation, who causes peaceable brothers to fight,
Yet who constantly gives friendship,
O mighty one, Lady of battle, who suppresses the mountains,
O Gushea, the one covered with fighting and clothed with terror
Thou dost make complete judgment and decision, the ordinances
of heaven and earth. . . .
O unequaled angry one of the fight, strong one in battle,
O firebrand which is kindled against the enemy, which brings about
the destruction of the furious (Prayer of Lamentation, quoted in
Ruether 1985:10).

Carol Christ is not unaware of this military side of the Goddess
but dismisses it as a patriarchal degeneration which must equally be
rejected "as liberating images for us today" (1987:80). This means, in
effect, that models of ancient Goddesses can be re-envisioned while
the model of the Hebrew deity must be renounced. YHWH's military
aspirations seem more intrinsic and indispensable to God's identity
than the allegedly more accidental and marginal violence of the
Goddess.

Ruether plays down the Goddess' militarism almost to the point
where it becomes a virtue. In *Womanguides*, Ruether carefully chooses
her words when presenting texts which laud a Goddess' military
prowess. The "Prayer of Lamentation to Ishtar," quoted above, appears
under the heading: "Ishtar, Shepherdess of the People" (1985:10).
Another text which celebrates Anat's military adventures is titled:
"Anat, Savior of Baal, Restores the World" (1985:107). The "Song of
Anat" opens with an enumeration of Anat's heroic deeds and recounts
the many enemies whom she previously "crushed, destroyed, muzzled,
cut off, fought, drove out, chased" away. She threatens to "fell" her
own father "like a lamb to the ground, [and] (make) his gray hair
(flow with) blood" should he deny helping her brother Baal who has
disappeared (Ruether 1985:113-114). Anat is reported to have enjoyed
walking "knee-deep in knight's blood, hip-deep in the gore of the
heroes" (S. Davies 1985:70). In her commentary Ruether lessens the
impact of Anat's violence and renders it a virtue. She notes that "we
feel immediately the enormous power and authority of Anat. She
commands the center of stage with her swift, decisive actions on
behalf of Baal and in confrontation with any power" (1985:106). Her
choice of words shifts the focus away from Anat's rage, intolerance

and violence and calls it "decisive" and "confrontational," virtues
which women are trying to emulate.

Ruether's interpretation of the Hebrew Bible, on the other hand,
heightens the impact of the soldier-like qualities of YHWH. Anat is
juxtaposed to "the male Warrior God of Israel and His son, the
Anointed one (Messiah), the King of Israel" who will come to restore
the kingdom and establish Israel "as the overlord of the world (the
Middle East)" (Ruether 1985:107). She chooses a passage from
Zechariah whose vision, according to her, summarizes "some of the
dreams of power and vengeance of Israelite messianism" (Ruether
1985:107). She leaves the reader with the impression that militarism
is an essential part of the biblical vision--and, perhaps not surprisingly,
she denounces Zionism in one of her later works (Ruether and Ruether
1989).

In the opposition between war and peace, Judaism is identified
with the former. This portrayal, again, ignores that the Jewish tradition
incorporates both sides. True, the people of Israel use military force
to attain a land which has been promised to them by YHWH. But the
biblical vision is one of peace and justice, specifically for the
oppressed. YHWH is pictured as Protector, Provider and Guide in
other than military ways. Imagery for YHWH encompasses feeding
and fighting, clothing and crying out, structuring daily life and
offering forgiveness. The warring, fighting, intolerant and harsh sides
of YHWH are balanced by compassion and love for people, by sorrow
over injustice and violence and by a willingness to hold back
judgment and destruction. If we must reject models from the past
because they contain oppressive and militarist elements, ancient
models of Goddesses have no inherent advantage. Both Christ and
Ruether deliberately minimize the importance of militarism for
Goddesses but amplify this characteristic for the Hebrew God.

German feminist Weiler's approach to YHWH as *Kriegsgott*
[wargod] differs from Christ and Ruether because she distinguishes
between a matriarchal YHWH and a patriarchal YHWH.[2] According
to her reading, Moses negotiates with the patriarchal YHWH up on
Mount Sinai, while the people left at the foot of the mountain worship
the matriarchal YHWH under the leadership of Aaron and Miriam as
the "bull of his mother," the male consort of the Canaanite Goddess

---

[2] See also Mulack who distinguishes between "*El Shaddai*" as the matriarchal
and "*YHWH Elohim*" as the patriarchal God (1983:144).

Anat. Only the patriarchal YHWH is militaristic, intolerant and outraged over the "ecstatic joy and orgiastic feast" among the people. He orders their murder:

> In contrast to the matriarchal Yahweh who had commanded: "Thou shalt not kill!" the patriarchal Yahweh appears powerfully and demands: "Put every man his sword on his side . . . and slay every man his brother, and every man his companion, and every man his neighbor (Ex 32:25)" (Weiler 1984:165).

The biblical tension between a peaceful and forgiving God versus an angry and violent God is split apart and attributed to two different traditions. Only the patriarchal YHWH is intolerant and commands the "extermination" of those who oppose him.[3] For Weiler, the patriarchal YHWH coincides with the Jewish God. Quoting a particularly anti-semitic statement by Mowinkel, she blends Jewish militarism with Nazi ideology:

> The kingdom of Yahweh is obviously supposed to be an empire which he reigns himself as king, while Israel supplies his civil servants, his court, and his *Herrenrasse* [masterrace]. . . . The content of the covenant [with God] is aimed at making Israel head and master over all peoples (Mowinkel, quoted in Weiler 1984:356).

For Weiler, the patriarchal YHWH desires world dominion and is determined to use any means necessary to attain it, including war, murder and the "cynical use of power."[4] The matriarchal YHWH, on the other hand, aims at harmonious and peaceful co-existence among and between people and uses war only for defensive purposes (1984:391).

---

[3] Carol Christ rejects "a form of monotheism that spawns religious intolerance and a climate in which destruction of people who practice other religions can be countenanced" (1987:79). Mulack finds Yahweh "tyrannical, jealous and vengeful" (1983:144); Stone protests "violent religious persecutions" and "commission of mass murder" (1978:187); Lerner maintains that the prophets "introduced into Yahwism the revolutionary idea of intolerance towards other gods and cults" (1986:166).

[4] The Israelite conquest of Canaan is deemed aggressive and unjust (Weiler 1984:259). For similar arguments, see Göttner-Abendroth 1980:79-82; Stone 1978:168.

The opposition of matriarchy versus patriarchy, peace versus war, confirms the rule of formation of antithesis and reasserts old gender roles which characterize men as strong, aggressive and destructive, while women are seen as weak, peace-loving and healing. This gender dualism has been critiqued by a variety of feminists (Thürmer-Rohr 1987:38-56; Harding 1986:163-197). Theologies that construct the "male" YHWH as militaristic and female Goddesses as peace-loving must be questioned for their anti-Jewish underpinnings.

YHWH as Lord and Lawgiver

Obedience to divine will receives sharply divergent evaluations depending on whether the author discusses submission to the Goddess or compliance with YHWH's word and law. While the Hebrew God emerges as an authoritarian dictator, compliance with the Goddess' requirements appears necessary and beneficial.

For example, Elga Sorge characterizes the God of Genesis as a dogmatic patriarch who is opposed to human freedom: "The God Yahweh formulates the authoritarian principle of incapacitation: those who want to know for themselves what is good or bad for [them]. . . have transgressed against the *Gesetzesgott* [God of law] and are expelled from paradise" (Sorge 1985:86; cf. Mulack 1983:42). In her interpretation God emerges as a tyrant who opposes independent thinking and decision-making and, instead, punishes maturity and self-determination. This characterization of YHWH enjoys particular popularity among German feminists.[5] They stress that YHWH's will and word are laid down in rigid laws which must be followed strictly and blindly. In their view, YHWH legitimizes authoritarianism and "law and order," and is therefore anachronistic to feminist values which espouse autonomy and individuality.

Jewish feminist Carol Ochs' reading of the *Akkedah*, the attempted sacrifice of Isaac, likewise dramatizes what she perceives to be the difference between matriarchal and patriarchal religion:

> The first allegiance in matriarchy is to one's offspring. . . . In patriarchy, the first obligation is to an abstract moral principle, the voice of God. The meaning of the test is that Abraham must prove

[5] Cf. Mulack 1983:139, 141, 230; Sorge 1985:83-89, 94, 146; Heine 1986:82-83; Weiler 1984:85, 334; Moltmann-Wendel 1986:167-179.

his allegiance under the new, patriarchal system. Abraham, after all, had challenged God once on the destruction of Sodom and Gomorrah (and saved his blood relative, Lot). In order to prove that Abraham is not rooted in the older tradition, God demands that he renounce the most fundamental tenet of the matriarchal religion and kill his own child (1977:45-46).

The content of Abraham's test is his "allegiance," or as Mulack put it, an exercise in "unconditional [and] slavish obedience" (1983:139, 141). A curious reversal takes place: Hebrew religion turns into a sacrificial religion which tests blind obedience at the expense of human life. Traditionally, the *Akkedah* was interpreted as the Hebrew God's rejection of child sacrifice. With the exception of Jephtah's daughter (Jgs 11:29-40), there is no account of ritual child sacrifice in the Hebrew Bible.[6] Abraham's readiness to sacrifice his son has traditionally been explained with reference to surrounding cultures which were supposed to have practiced child sacrifice. Daum and McCauley point out that,

according to the Jewish tradition, the crucial moral truth revealed is God's **opposition** to human sacrifice. This contrasts with ritual sacrifice of the male consort of the High Priestess in Goddess worship of pre-biblical days, a matter overlooked by Ochs and Stone. It also contrasts with the Christian theological focus which depicts Christ as the "Lamb of God" whose sacrifice is **required** (1983:179).

While Ochs seems to ignore matriarchal sacrifices, other feminist theologians acknowledge sacrificial practices but present them sympathetically, if not approvingly. For Weiler, matriarchal sacrifice is performed in accordance with "nature." The same event appears here as a beneficial and enlightened submission to the laws of nature.

The matriarchal person lived tied in with nature--not because he (*sic*) lived unconsciously . . . but because he consciously submitted to the wisdom of matriarchal creative power. . . . The death of nature is dramatized by the matriarchal person through death of the

---

[6] Mulack asserts that "the Bible shows, that mass murders of children are no rarity, and represent, so to speak, as the `wrath of God' the other side of the loving Father God" (1985:159). Elizabeth Gould Davis surmises that God's acceptance of Abel's meat sacrifice means that the harmony between humans and animals is broken and that death and destruction have become commonplace (1971:136).

cultic king and his journey into the underworld: during harvest time
. . . the king has to die as well, be it in the cultic process of actual
killing, be it in symbolic cultic drama (1984:29; cf. Göttner-
Abendroth 1983:171-195).

The anti-Jewish prejudice is apparent when one compares the
phrasing of Weiler and Ochs. Weiler attempts to redeem matriarchal
sacrifice by coding it as a wise and necessary submission to nature.
Less dramatic events in the Hebrew Bible, on the other hand, are
depicted in such a way as to cause outrage and protest against "blind
faith" and fearful docility.

I would think, however, that neither "matriarchal" nor
"patriarchal" obedience can be understood without their theological
center. "Sacrifices" are necessary to move towards a goal. The Hebrew
God promises freedom, justice and peace and asks for obedience in
order to move people closer to that goal. Likewise, Weiler's and
Göttner-Abendroth's matriarchal sacrifice becomes meaningful only if
one accepts the Goddess' promise of safe passage through winter into
spring and a year of plenty. Without these promises, the required
submissions make no sense. Unfortunately, some matriarchal
reconstructions are preceded by value judgments, praising one side and
denigrating the other. With the same legitimacy with which the
obedience to YHWH's law is described as submission to a totalitarian
dictator, the sacrifice of the king in Goddess religion can be
considered murder. Do antithetical descriptions of the Hebrew God
really serve feminist appropriations of Goddess spirituality?

YHWH as Bodiless Otherworldly God

A third antithesis in feminist writings about the Goddess occurs
when the nature-culture split is applied to Hebrew religion. Nature,
plants, animals and the human body are valued highly in feminist
writings because women have traditionally been identified with nature
and sexuality (Griffin 1978; Ortner 1974; Griscom 1985:85-98). In
some instances, Judaism becomes identified with the opposite side,
namely culture. This is particularly ironic in light of traditional
Christian anti-Judaism which assigned Judaism a place among the
lower, material realm of nature, while Christianity was considered
enlightened and spiritual (Boyarin 1993:1-10). Gnostic Christians like
the third century heretic Marcion rejected the Jewish God because he
had created and blessed earth and nature (Ruether 1974a:51-52). In

some scholarship on the Goddess, the same Jewish God is now perceived to be above creation, an otherworldly, bodiless divinity, responsible for giving permission to humanity to "fill the earth and subdue it; and have dominion over . . . every living thing that moves upon the earth" (Gn 1:28). Sheila Collins writes that

> the first scapegoat to fall sway to the drive of patriarchal monotheism for predominance in the ancient world was the organic interrelationship of humanity with nature and concomitantly, the role and importance of woman. As we have seen the natural world is demeaned. It was no longer the locus of the numinous, the sacred, but an inferior `order' of creation which man was to dominate and subdue (1974:140).

Once again, Hebrew patriarchal monotheism is rendered the antithesis, this time of the ecology movement, by being blamed for the destruction of the "organic interrelationship of humanity with nature."

The nature-culture split, however, is promoted most forcefully in Greek philosophy. Greek assertions of the soul/spirit's superiority over the physical/material realm are not supported by the biblical tradition which, by and large, does not understand the quest for transcendence as a flight from nature and the body. The divine is known in and through nature, immanent in the physical world as well as transcendent to it. Biblical language uses rich metaphors from the agricultural and natural world to refer to God and Israel without reducing either to it.

Several feminist theologians (Ochs 1977:47; Collins 1974:63; Ruether 1979a:47; Mulack 1983:139; Ochshorn 1985:17) maintain that Goddess religions express greater affinity and harmony with nature and sexuality: "What was happening in the transition from a polytheistic matriarchal world view to a monotheistic patriarchal system was a reversal of values" (Collins 1974:140). They argue that matriarchal religions celebrate fertility, sexuality and nature, while Hebrew monotheism rejects them. This portrayal patently overlooks the fact that fertility of the land and the people of Israel are a central concern to biblical religion. Against such reversals, Hackett warns that by "embracing rather than rejecting the `fertility religion' that is pre-sented as rival of the official religion of Israel, they [feminists] think they are defying the male-centered religion of Israel and of the scholars who write the secondary literature" (1989:68). She suggests avoiding these dualistic oppositions altogether by critiquing androcentric accounts which have elevated Israelite religion to the higher, cultural, spiritual realm, and have polemicized against pagan religions as nature and fertility religion.

Male Monotheism

Some feminists argue that patriarchal monotheism is more exclusive of women than polytheistic religions because the divine realm is purged of female images and attributes. The Hebrew God is described as exclusively male and then repudiated as the ultimate expression of patriarchal religion, ostracizing women theologically and symbolically. For Gerda Lerner, monotheism is the ultimate form of patriarchal religion:

> It remains for the pantheon of gods to be replaced by one single powerful male God and for that God to incorporate the principle of generativity in both of its aspects. This shift, which occurs in many different forms in different cultures, occurs for the Western civilization in the Book of Genesis (1986:180).

The argument of "male monotheism" deliberately ignores monotheism's claim to worship a God without image and gender (cf. Wacker 1987a:114-125). It denies the existence of other metaphors and the theological option to create new symbols in monotheism. Phyllis Trible, for instance, maintains that the Hebrew God is not exclusively male. YHWH's masculinity is as much a product of translation and interpretation as of actual biblical language. Stripping away layers of androcentric interpretation, Trible finds images such as:

> Midwife, seamstress, housekeeper, nurse, and mother: all these feminine images characterize Yahweh, the God of Israel. . . . Although the Old Testament often pictures Yahweh as a man, it also uses gynomorphic language for the deity. At the same time, Israel repudiated the idea of sexuality in God. Unlike fertility gods, Yahweh is neither male nor female; neither he nor she. Consequently, modern assertions that God is masculine, even when they are qualified, are misleading and detrimental, if not altogether inaccurate. Cultural and grammatical limitations (the use of masculine pronouns for God) need not limit theological under-standing (1973:34).

Goddess theologies which reduce monotheism to monolatry, that is, to a single image of God as male, ignore the variety of biblical metaphors and leave the impression that the creation of patriarchy and monotheism coincide. Patriarchy, however, developed independently of monotheism and polytheism. The ideology of male supremacy shapes polytheistic, monotheistic and nontheistic religions (as well as atheistic ideologies) in different ways. The presence of female symbols for the divine does not necessarily indicate the absence of male supremacy and patriarchal social relations. Indeed, female symbols can be powerful patriarchal tools to keep women in place. The ancient Babylonian, Mesopotamian, Canaanite, Greek and Roman pantheons of gods and goddesses, existing prior to, and at the same time as, biblical monotheism, supported male supremacy and reinforced patriarchal values. The chain of historical events, as depicted by Gerda Lerner in *The Creation of Patriarchy,* is anti-Jewish because it singles out biblical faith as the ultimate expression of patriarchal religion.

In this chapter, I have examined representations of Hebrew society and religion in feminist scholarship on the Goddess. I discovered that this research emphasizes oppressive and reprehensible aspects of the Hebrew faith in order to make Goddess religion more attractive. As in Christian feminist writings, Goddess thealogies use Jewish monotheism as a screen onto which attributes and values considered destructive and troublesome are projected. Judaism becomes a signifier for the enemy. The rule of formation of antithesis asserts itself in quasi-historical approaches which use ancient models of Goddesses as a basis of feminist Goddess spirituality.

Chapter VI

JUDAISM AS SCAPEGOAT FOR PATRIARCHY

In the preceding chapters I documented antithetical representations of Judaism in Christian and post-Christian feminist writings. This chapter will examine whether Judaism is blamed for the creation of patriarchal evils. The rule of formation of scapegoat goes beyond depicting Judaism as a religion inferior to Christianity and paganism, blaming it for various ills in this world. Specifically, Judaism is faulted for the origin of sexism and patriarchy. It is singled out and made responsible for the destruction of Goddess worship and blamed for the persecution and death of the feminist, matriarchal Jesus.

THE FALL FROM PARADISE

Theologians who postulate the harmonious existence of pre-historical matriarchal religions have to account for their destruction and loss. Since matriarchies are seen as utopian, paradisiacal places, modern narratives of their destruction tend to have somewhat mythic overtones. To some extent, narratives of matriarchy's downfall parallel Christian accounts of humanity's expulsion from paradise. Like Adam and Eve's Fall, the rise of patriarchy is depicted as a loss of original harmony and a deterioration into alienation, strife, evil and injustice. While the traditional myth held Eve responsible for being the "devil's gateway," the patriarchal Hebrews now take on her role. Judaism becomes the scapegoat in the myth of the Fall from matriarchy into patriarchy.

Several authors focus in their critique of patriarchal religion on the Hebrew Bible and attribute the shift from matriarchal to patriarchal religion to Hebrew monotheism (Sorge 1985:22; Göttner-Abendroth 1980:82; Weiler 1984:392; Stone 1982:68; S. Collins 1974:68, 76,

119-122). Marga Monheim-Geffert, for example, assumes that "what begins with Abraham is the male story of the male God with his male followers on earth, and that was something completely new" (1982:200). But patriarchy had already been established when Israelite religion emerged. The end of matriarchal religion and the origin of patriarchal religion is falsely attributed to Hebrew religion. The isolation of Hebrew monotheism as the ultimate step in the development of patriarchal religion is misleading and anti-Jewish in its consequence.

In *The Creation of Patriarchy*, Gerda Lerner offers a comprehensive historical account of this process in the ancient Near East. For her, the Book of Genesis "is the historical moment of the death of the Mother-Goddess and her replacement by God-the-Father and the metaphorical Mother under patriarchy" (1986:198). Her chronology of patriarchy's development highlights the Hebrew Scriptures in a way that is neither historically valid nor theologically warranted. While her historical analysis is usually sensitive to issues of power, she fails to see that the small Israelite cult of YHWH could not have undermined the religious authority of the Egyptian Isis, Greek Aphrodite, Roman Venus and Assyrian Myllita (1986:159). While YHWH's sphere of influence may have impacted on the Canaanite Goddesses Anat and Asherah, it is implausible to assume that religious movements in Palestine impressed the empires of Egypt, Babylonia, Greece, Assyria and Rome. The diminishing influence and power of Goddesses throughout the Near East and Mediterranean area were caused by factors unrelated to Hebrew monotheism. Lerner, whose analysis of gender, race and class relations in ancient societies is generally astute, seems not to recognize Israel's inability to influence the religious make up of surrounding empires. By focusing almost exclusively on the Hebrew Bible in her analysis of patriarchal religious ideology she assigns an improper share of responsibility to Hebrew monotheism and, thus, perpetuates anti-Judaism.

Similarly, Charlene Spretnak, who is primarily concerned with Greek Goddesses in her book *Lost Goddesses of Early Greece* (1978), refers repeatedly to the Hebrew Bible when explaining the destruction of matriarchal religion. She creates the impression that the implementation of Hebrew patriarchy preceded Greek patriarchy. For instance, Spretnak juxtaposes biblical monotheism with Minoan Goddess worship, although the former clearly had no influence on the latter.

The Goddess religion and its `pagan' worshipers were brutally
destroyed in Biblical lands. The Old Testament is the military and
cultural record (albeit considerably laundered) of a massive
political coup. It is important to note that we did not emerge into
patriarchal religion from a dark, chaotic, immature period of
primitivism; Goddess-centered cultures, including Minoan Crete,
were highly evolved (1978:29).

Spretnak is right about Minoan Crete's high civilization, but is
the same true for the Palestinian highlands (cf. Meyers 1988:50-71)?
Can the fall of Minoan Crete be explained with reference to the
Hebrew Bible? Greece was firmly patriarchal before Hebrew religion
emerged. How can the "Old Testament" be the record of the
destruction of Greek Goddesses? As Carol Christ has pointed out,
Greece became patriarchal during the fourth, third and second
millennia B.C.E. (1987:75). The Israelite Exodus from Egypt, the first
historically verifiable event in the Hebrew Bible, occurred around
1275-1250 B.C.E. and the biblical texts were written and compiled
sometime during the first millennium B.C.E. (Seltzer 1980:7-34).
Greek as well as Canaanite Goddesses, to whom Spretnak refers, were
embedded in patriarchal cultures. They had slowly been integrated,
seduced and subjugated into a patriarchal polytheistic pantheon before
the monotheistic battle against "idolatry" had even begun. Monotheism
is not *per definitionem* more patriarchal than the polytheistic pantheon,
the latter distorting and changing the images of female deities into
heavenly examples of patriarchal, earthly gender relations. Did the
monotheistic battle against these patriarchal images of femininity
perhaps appeal to women? The equation of patriarchy with
monotheism and matriarchy with polytheism identifies Judaism as
culprit in the creation of patriarchy.

According to Spretnak the Goddess religion of biblical lands is
overthrown by a "massive political coup" and "brutally destroyed"
(1978:29). Matriarchal religions, she contends, did not become
obsolete but were repressed by brute force. In the same vein, Carol
Christ explains that "settled matrilineal and relatively peaceful societies in Greece and the Mediterranean area were conquered and/or
assimilated by patrilineal, patriarchal and warlike invaders during the
fourth, third and second millennia B.C.E." (1987:75). Other authors
variously identify the biblical "invaders" as "Northern invaders"
(Ochshorn 1981:10), "Indo-Europeans" (Stone 1978:62-128), "semitic
conquerors" (Ruether 1985:4), "male God invaders" (Swidler 1979:23)
or as "an order of fanatical priests of Yahweh who probably came

from the South" (Weiler 1984:81).These characterizations imply that matriarchies became victims of hostile, violent forces rather than of an internal lack or failure to supply meaning and a satisfying *Welt-anschauung*.

The association of the Hebrews with an epithet such as "semitic conquerors" is disturbing. Given medieval and modern stereotypes of the Wandering Jew who is condemned to endure exile and homelessness, the suggestion of a Hebrew patriarchal invasion of Canaan is politically charged. It contributes to images of Jews as hostile outsiders whose presence and influence is perceived as destructive (Hasan-Rokem and Dundes 1986). For example, Stone's description of the Hebrew settlement of Canaan may be a correct rendition of certain strands within the Bible, but read in a modern context, her phrasing is reminiscent of anti-Zionist ideology.

> The Bible account admits that Canaan was already inhabited and that many of the people lived in great fortified towns. Despite this, we read of the intention of the arriving Hebrews not only to continue into the land of Canaan, but to purposely and violently destroy the existing religion and replace it with their own (1978:169).

Such language betrays an affinity to antisemitism which dreaded the Jews as conspirators and infiltrators who planned to dominate and oppress indigenous populations. Especially after the Holocaust, such imagery is dangerous.[1] The biblical account is an oversimplification. A one-time conquest of Canaan by the Hebrews as described in Joshua is debated among biblical scholars on historical grounds (Bright 1975:130-133; Orlinsky 1960:45ff). It is more likely that Israelite settlement of Canaan was a combination of acculturation and warfare by various tribal groups over an extended period of time. Stone's sympathies lie with the Canaanites whom she characterizes as a people who lived in peace and prosperity until attacked by a territorial and religious aggressor. Her hermeneutic choice occurs because she identifies Canaanite culture with matriarchy and ignores the fact that

---

[1] For Stone the Holocaust is "not only . . . tragic but . . . ironic" (1978:68-69). She imagines Hitler to mean "teacher of Hit(tites)" and derives the term Nazi from "the Hebrew word *nasi* for prince" (Stone 1978:127). These false and ridiculous claims strengthen her thesis of a close connection between the "Indo-European peoples . . . [and] the extreme patriarchal attitudes of the Hebrews" (1978:68-69), thereby merging the victims of the Holocaust with the perpetrators.

the Canaanites were a patriarchal culture, militarily superior to the Hebrews.

Clearly the biblical narrative of the conquest of the land is troubling in its one-sided mythologizing. Yet, reversing the partiality by embracing the Canaanites as a peaceful matriarchal culture attacked by Hebrew invaders leaves the mythology intact. In light of traditional depictions of Jews as "outside invaders" this feminist representation of the Hebrews as "semitic conquerors" adds to the scapegoating of Jews as a sinister force in the world.

FALLING BACK INTO PATRIARCHY

While some neo-pagan feminists blame the Israelites for the violent overthrow of matriarchy, some Christian feminists explain Christian patriarchy as a *"Rückfall"* [return] (Mulack 1983:325) or "fall[ing] back" (Parvey 1974:127) into patriarchy which, invariably, means Jewish patriarchy. Elisabeth Gössman detects a "rejudaization . . . around the end of the first century when the eschatological expectation did not fulfill itself" (1983:52). More subtly, Moltmann-Wendel suspects that sexism in the New Testament is the result of a "Jewish-Christian redaction" (1977:14) or, as Wolff puts it, a "Jewish-Christian retouching" (1979:133). Moltmann-Wendel locates patriarchal resistance in "difficulties, which the Jewish-Christian congregations create for the new women's movement" (1980:133). Pagels, based on Leipoldt, explains the increasing patriarchalization in Christian communities with "the influx of many Hellenized Jews into the movement [which] may have influenced the church in the direction of Jewish traditions" (1979:76). Without consciously intending to so, some feminists end up blaming Judaism for the Christian Fall into patriarchy.

The issue of menstrual taboos is a case in point. Menstrual taboos are oftentimes explained with reference to the purity laws of the Hebrew Bible. While, on the surface, the reference to the Hebrew Bible is accurate, the assumption of a "cultural lag" minimizes the responsibility of those church fathers who introduced new repressive social codes in the church. A number of Christian authors argue that Jesus abolished menstrual taboos when he healed the hemorrhaging woman after she touched his cloak (Mk 5:25-34) (Mollenkott 1977:14; Moltmann-Wendel 1980:106-107; Heine 1986:77; Jewett 1975:102;

Ruether 1975:71; Mulack 1983:279; Wolff 1979:127; Oepke 1957:785). Ruether contends in *New Woman New Earth*:

> Jewish law regarded a woman with a flow of blood as unclean and polluting anyone whom she touched. Jesus' reaction to the woman with a hemorrhage shows his deliberate discarding of this taboo, while the woman's own terror at being discovered in touching his garment reveals her awareness of having violated this taboo (Mark 5:25-34; Matt. 9:20-22; Luke 8:43-48) (1975:65).

Since Jesus never expressly opposed *Niddah*, laws regarding menstruation, one may question the conclusion that "by immediate implication . . . [Jesus] rejected the concept of the `uncleanness' of a woman who had a flow of blood" (Swidler 1979:181). But, if indeed, menstrual taboos were suspended in the early church, we have to ask when and why were they reinstituted.

The controversy over whether menstruating women should be barred from receiving the Eucharist began in the third century C.E. Can inner-Christian debates of the third century be explained (away) as "a regression" (Jewett 1975:105) or "an unwitting application of priestly-ritual practices of the past" (Stagg and Stagg 1978:32) or a revival of "Old Testament laws of purity" (Ruether 1975:65)? Swidler contends that "Dionysius forbade Christian women from entering a church during their menstruation" because he held on "to the Hebraic laws of ritual impurity, which Jesus rejected" (1979:343). In each case, the Christian introduction of menstrual discrimination is explained with reference to the church's Hebrew-Jewish past.

This strategy deflects from the ethical and political responsibility of those Christian leaders who chose to emphasize repressive aspects of the Hebrew (and/or Hellenist) traditions while ignoring liberating practices in these heritages. Bishop Dionysius, who was responsible for the institution of menstrual discrimination, was born to pagan parents in Alexandria in the third century C.E. He elaborates his position that menstruating women should not be admitted to receive the Eucharist without mention of Jewish purity laws. Very matter-of-factly he assumes that no woman would be "rash enough in such a condition to approach the holy table or to touch the body and blood of Christ" (Kraemer 1988:43). Without further explanation he refers to the "time of their separation" (i.e. menstruation): apparently menstrual constraints were widely observed in Alexandria quite independently from Hebrew or rabbinic ritual law.

Dionysius was a contemporary of the *Amoraim*, the rabbis who commented on the Mishnah. Their obsessive concern with women's purity could have been caused by the same cultural and political forces that supported the conservative, priestly orientation of the church. A conservative backlash during the third and fourth centuries may have affected both the rabbis and church fathers and each tradition must be held accountable for its patriarchal choices. Christians, however, tend to shift their share of the responsibility onto Judaism, as does Sheila Collins when she argues that taboos and ritual uncleanness "were incorporated in the Torah and Talmud and from there passed on into Christianity" (1974:74). She portrays Judaism as older and therefore responsible for patriarchy. Her statement vindicates Christianity: it received passively what was "passed on" or, as Stagg and Stagg put it, "applied unwittingly" what already existed (1978:32). Christianity is depicted as a powerless and innocent victim of a sexist Jewish past rather than active and responsible shaper of a new patriarchal tradition. The power of sexism is underestimated; Christianity's choices, mistakes and failures are glossed over. Calling the Christian backlash a return to Judaism renders Judaism the scapegoat. The "Jewish-cultural-lag-theory" of Christian sexism permits Christians to erase the profound ambiguity and alienation from their spiritual home. Instead, patriarchy is presented as a containable and defeatable regression of Christianity. The Jewish scapegoat assumes the burden of responsibility and serves to reconcile feminist and Christian identities.

MATRICIDE

The myth of the "Hebrew patriarchal invaders" and the "Jewish cultural lag" present socio-historical reasons for the disappearance of matriarchy and feminist Christianity. Claims about the murder of the Goddess express the disappearance of matriarchal religions theologically (cf. Collins 1974:124; Sorge 1985:53; Mulack 1983:248, 271, 275; Stone 1982:14, 21; Chicago 1982:153; Christ 1987:24; Lerner 1986:198). Several Jewish feminists raised their voices against the popular notion that "the Jews killed the Goddess" because they consider it a disturbing resurrection of the deicide charge (Daum 1982; Heschel 1986, 1988; Goldstein 1986). It is not difficult to see how the traditional charges that "the Jews killed Christ" and the representation of Jews as "Christkillers" parallel post-Christian depictions of Hebrew monotheism as a merciless, brutal and intolerant religion which persecuted and destroyed the Goddess. Christian characterizations of the Jews as a people who would rather demand Christ's death than give up their blind and obstinate faith in a rigid and narrow-minded Law are transferred to the Goddess. German feminist Gerda Weiler argues that

> patriarchal monotheism develops over the elimination of the cosmic mistress: There is no "Father in Heaven" without "Matricide!". . . The theological speculation which wants to project Yahweh as sole God and creator of all things to the beginning of all times, originates with the Levites at the Jerusalem temple. They deface matriarchal ritual texts, polemicize against the Heavenly Queen and lead a merciless battle against matriarchal social practice in Judah (1984:103).

Weiler blames biblical monotheism for the death of the Goddess although there is no reference to the killing of a Goddess in the Hebrew Scriptures. This is quite different in other Near Eastern and Mediterranean cultures where myths of murder, rape and marriage of Goddesses abound. The Babylonian Genesis story, the *Enuma Elish*, records the murder and dismemberment of the Goddess Tiamat by her son Marduk (cf. Daly 1978:107). Likewise, Greek mythology explains the Goddesses' loss of power in stories of Zeus's marriages, rapes and murders. Yet, the Hebrew Bible remains silent. Indeed, religious polemics in the Hebrew Bible are mainly directed against the male God Baal. Most confrontations between Canaanite and Hebrew religions occur between the male fertility God Baal and YHWH. Goddess "idols" seem to have been tolerated (Patai 1967) until the prophets directed their attention to them (Jer 44:15). The biblical battle against "idolatry" affected male and female "idols" alike and should not be referred to as "Goddess murder."

In addition, the "merciless battle" was fought internally and did not affect neighboring patriarchal cultures. YHWH claimed loyalty only from Israelites without disputing the legitimate existence of other Gods and Goddesses for other communities (cf. the first commandment in Ex 20:3). Israel's election can be interpreted as a covenant with YHWH that is particular and does not impose on other ethnic communities. Only when Israelites began to worship "idols" was the fury of YHWH and the prophets unleashed. This kind of intra-group religious intolerance must be understood in the context of Israel's powerlessness and struggle for survival surrounded by expansionist empires. Israel did not have the power (even if it had the desire) to enforce its religion on other cultures.

This outlook changed when Christian monotheism sought universal acceptance of the one trinitarian God. As Carol Christ noted correctly, the suppression of Goddess worship extended over many centuries and well into the fourth century of the Common Era when the Roman Empire adopted Christianity as its official religion. "Christian culture waged its own campaign against `paganism' and `heresy' in which the suppression of female symbolism for the divine was a factor. . . . It was later Christian emperors who passed laws allowing for the destruction of pagan temples, including Goddess temples in the Christian empire" (1987:87). Indeed, the laws of Constantine (337-361 C.E.) and, in particular, the *Codex Theodosianus* (438 C.E.) legally enforced Christian supremacy by declaring it the only catholic, that is universal, licit religion of the Roman Empire. All other religions were outlawed except Judaism which alone was granted limited rights and a chance of survival (Marcus 1981:3-12). The responsibility for the death of the Goddess should be placed at the door of Christianity.

The charge of Goddess murder leveled against Jewish monotheism is disturbing because of the sacpegoating at work. Historical narratives which bypass pagan and Christian responsibilities for the marginalization of Goddess worship blame Judaism. The accusation that the Hebrews rather than the Greeks, Babylonians or Romans killed the Goddess is more compelling to the Christian mind because it fits neatly into the long tradition of deicide charges and the stereotype of the Jews as "Christkillers." Interestingly, this charge has also begun to influence Christian feminist depictions of Jesus' death.

DEICIDE

As mentioned earlier, some Christian authors maintain that Jesus restored matriarchy and reinstated the values attributed to matriarchal religions. Jesus championed egalitarianism, justice, peace, liberation and harmony between the sexes, races and classes. Women found respect, authority, leadership opportunities and dignity in the Jesus movement. Because of these visions and values, Jesus had to die.

Elga Sorge elaborates upon this connection. She combines the death of the Goddess with the death of Jesus and argues that the matriarchal male Jesus "was convicted by Jewish priests for blasphemy

. . . because he placed the force of the Goddess above Yahweh's claims for subjugation. Jesus did the worst one can possibly do from a Jewish point of view: he dethroned Yahweh" (1985:123). The matriarchal Jesus speaks in the name of the Goddess and reinstates the old religion. Ironically, "old" no longer refers to the outdated "Old Testament," but to matriarchy which predates Hebrew monotheism. Jesus invalidates Yahweh and renders patriarchal Judaism obsolete.

> Jesus has reopened the door to paradise which Yahweh had locked as a punishment. . . . Thus Jesus has shaken off the yoke of the patriarchal god who demands submission and obedience and has replaced it with the light burden and gentle yoke of cosmic love and paradisiacal freedom which nourishes all those who labor and are heavy laden instead of torturing them with legal obligations (Sorge 1985:123).

Sorge reinterprets the classic Christian paradigm of fall and redemption from a feminist perspective. But she adds a distinctly anti-Jewish twist. In her scheme, Judaism has never possessed any revelatory truth and rightness, not before, during or after the coming of Christ. While traditional theology at least admitted some truth to Jewish revelation before the coming of Christ, and later replaced Israel's covenantal relationship to God with the church, Sorge dispenses with the Hebrew Bible and Jewish existence altogether. For her, Judaism represents a decline from earlier matriarchal religion that continues to be obstinate and blind to matriarchal values--until it is eventually overcome by Jesus' reaffirmation of matriarchal religion. Sorge almost denies Jesus' Jewishness: "The son of man is not a Jewish Messiah but a matriarchal Heros figure" (1985:122). This statement evokes both Marcion's "Gnostic Christ" as well as Nazi theologian Grundmann's "Aryan Jesus" (1940). Sorge's matriarchal and anti-Jewish Jesus proclaims the end of patriarchy which coincides with the end of the Old Testament and Judaism. Sorge's theology seems particularly blatant because she identifies Judaism entirely with patriarchal evil and denies its validity and legitimacy at any point.

Some feminist reclamations of Mary, the Mother of God, point to similarities between Mary and ancient Goddesses, and understand Mary's influential position in the church as a resurrection of the Goddess. Others describe Jesus as the Son of the Goddess comparable to the matriarchal son-lover-consort of the Goddess. Both Ruether's "Kenosis of the Father" (1983:1-11) and Collins' "A Tale of Two Deities" (1974:25-30) proclaim Jesus as the Son of the older, pre-patriarchal Goddess, reasserting matriarchal religion over against the reign of the patriarchal God. Spretnak suggests that "the Virgin Mary is clearly rooted in the older Goddess religion because she produces her child parthenogenetically. (And Jesus himself is true to the older pattern of the Goddess' son/lover dying at the spring equinox and being reborn at the Winter Solstice)" (1978:30; cf. Ochs 1977:81; Sorge 1985:59). Although both Judaism and Christianity appropriate and reevaluate "pagan" symbols, only Christianity represents a revitalization of matriarchy while Judaism is blamed for the destruction of matriarchal symbols. Judaism "usurped and perverted" (Göttner-Abendroth 1980:82), "transformed and reversed" (Ruether 1989:152), "coopted and inverted" (Spretnak 1978:29), "transmuted" (Lerner 1986:192) and "rewrote" (Mulack 1983:138) matriarchal symbols. Christianity, on the other hand, "restores," "reopens" (Sorge 1985:123) or "is rooted" in matriarchy (Spretnak 1978:30).

As a messenger of matriarchy, the opponents of Jesus and the Goddess merge. Jesus dies at the hands of those who killed the Goddess. Because Jesus is portrayed as the representative of a more authentic and older tradition, he shares the fate of the "Great Mother." Collins, for instance, specifies that "the Great King's followers hated him for this [i.e. his teachings], and they put him to death. He went back to his mother's womb, from whence he emerged and appeared to some women" (1974:29). Though not spelled out explicitly, the followers of the "Great King" are, in all likelihood, the Jews.

Mulack brackets Judaism as an isolated patriarchal religion and fuses the death of the Goddess with the death of Christ:

> That which the Jews had slowly extinguished in century-long battles is now celebrating its resurrection with Mary and Jesus: Anat and Baal, Cybele and Attis, Ishtar and Tummuz, Inanna and Dummuzi, Isis and Osiris, Hathor and Horus, Nut and Re, Aphrodite and Adonis, Artemis and Aktaion, Anahita and Mitra, Sarasvati and Brahma, Shakti and Shiva, Lakshmi and Vishnu, Dana and Dagda, Erin and Lug, Freya and Freyr, Frigga and Od Baldur--innumerable are the names of the Mother Goddesses and her son/lover who extend through all cultures of the earth and through all eons (1983:271).

Reminiscent of a Jewish world conspiracy, Mulack blames the Jews for the destruction of matriarchal religions in all cultures and eons. At the same time, Christianity is exempted from responsibility and claimed as legitimate heir of "matriarchal" religion. Christianity displaces Judaism now dispossessed of religious truth and charged with a double deicide: the Goddess and her "deputy" Jesus. In their opposition to, and victimization by, Judaism, matriarchy and Jesus unite. The Jewish scapegoat redeems Christianity as an anti-patriarchal and feminist religion.

Like these matriarchal-christological interpretations, more traditional Christian feminist interpretations of Christ's death have also not abandoned the anti-Jewish portrayal of Jesus' trial and conviction. They accentuate and dramatize Jesus' unique feminism by relying on classic understandings of Jesus' conviction over religious differences. His death solidifies his solidarity with women who are also persecuted and victimized by patriarchal forces. The reasons for Jesus' death reflect the theological agendas of the authors. According to McFague, Jesus' table fellowship with sinners and unclean people was reason enough to kill him.

> One did not eat with the ritually unclean, with Gentiles, with those in despised trades; hence for Jesus to eat with such peoples, to be called the `friend' of such people, was a scandal to most people as well as a form of radical acceptance for his friends at table. Jeremias and Perrin agree that such a practice alone was sufficient cause for his being put to death on a cross, for it shattered the Jews' attempt to close ranks against the Roman enemy by keeping the community pure (1982:181).

According to Sorge, Jesus died "because he loved women" (1985:77); according to Swidler, Jesus "led women astray" which "so infuriated the men that they publicly denounced Jesus for it to the Roman governor and demanded that he be executed. . . . Jesus' feminism was perceived as a capital crime" (1979:177). For Mulack, Jesus' defense of the adulterous woman (Jn 8:7) "provided them [i.e. Jews] with the justification to get rid of him" (1983:294). Moltmann-Wendel suggests that Jesus "violates family duties, in a way which according to the Old Testament calls for the death penalty" (1986:100).[2]

---

[2] Psychological discourse of repression and inability to deal with one's "shadow" provides a new rationale for deicide: "The pious simply refuse to be confronted with their shadow--as so many patients in therapy! . . . Thus acts desperate and blind self-defense, the brutality of obstinacy stuck in a shadow situation. . . . Jesus' crucifixion is the most extreme and consequent separation from the collective shadow" (Wolff 1979:128).

If one contemplates the probability of the assumption that Jews would convict a fellow Jew because he was a feminist, because he ate with the wrong people or violated family duties, the subtext of these charges becomes apparent: they undermine the moral and religious legitimacy of Judaism. What kind of a religion and what kind of law would kill an innocent and good person for such reasons? Such argumentation betrays a deep-seated suspicion towards Judaism and augments the perception of Judaism as evil. It lends new legitimacy to the old charge of deicide by adding feminism to the list of religious infractions which led to Jesus' death.

The authors may not consciously intend to blame Judaism for patriarchy or deicide. Anti-Judaism occurs because theological concerns introduce biases in favor of Christian or pagan religions. If one compares Ruether's *Faith and Fratricide* (1974a) with *Sexism and God-Talk* (1983), one can see how her accounts of Jesus' opponents change in her later work because of her theological agenda. In *Faith and Fratricide*, Ruether argues that "we find an extraordinary need in the Gospels to shift the blame for the deaths of Jesus and his disciples away from Roman political authority to Jewish religious authority" (1974a:88). She explains this shift with the exigencies of early Christian missionizing and survival needs in Rome. The early church found itself in a beleaguered and apologetic position towards the Gentile world. The memory of Jesus as a political martyr put the Christian community at great risk, and the evangelists took pains to emphasize that Jesus had been acquitted by Pilate and the Roman authorities in order to minimize Roman suspicions concerning the new cult. However, the Gospel writers shifted the blame "not only upon Jewish (much less Gentile) political authority but specifically upon the head of the Jewish religious tradition and its authority" (Ruether 1974a:88). This, Ruether maintains, was intended to disqualify the rival religion of Judaism. By blaming the death of an innocent man on the Jewish religion, Judaism lost respect among potential Gentile converts. In her historical analysis Ruether critically investigates the circumstances of Jesus' death and takes the theological and political agendas which informed the Gospel writers' memory into account.

In *Sexism and God-Talk*, published nine years later, Ruether moves from an historical to a theological approach to the New Testament. She speaks in Jesus' voice, imagines herself in his personality and describes his opponents as they are characterized by the Gospels--this time, neglecting the particular interests and additions of the evangelists:

> Although Jesus is aware of the oppressive Roman powers as the
> ultimate context of oppression, he focuses instead on the Jewish
> ruling classes--the local rulers, landlords, and religious authorities.
> He directs his criticism particularly at the religious authorities. It
> is they who have excluded, through their law- and class-based
> religion, the "little ones" from hope of redemption (1983:120).

Because a theological agenda informs this historical reconstruction, the
anti-Jewish polemic of the Gospels reappears. The critical historical
distance from the polemic distortions of the Gospels is lost, and the
conflict paradigm of the New Testament is used theologically--the
"little ones" are contrasted with a "law-and class-based religion."
Contradicting her earlier position in *Faith and Fratricide*, she portrays
Jesus in direct and irreconcilable conflict with the religious authorities
of his days. Although Ruether does not explicitly blame Jewish
religious authorities for Jesus' death, it is they who have a vested
interest in his death and presumably had to alert the Roman political
authorities--exactly as the New Testament accounts suggest. His death
is portrayed as the inevitable consequence of his opposition to
Judaism, and Jews are, once again, entangled in deicide.

THE ORIGIN OF PATRIARCHY AND EVIL

As the originators of patriarchy, Jews are uniquely responsible
for various social ills. Based on the Christian paradigm of the Fall
which maintains that humanity lost its innocence after the Fall and
was rendered fundamentally alienated from God, fellow humans and
nature, patriarchy is also seen as having irreversibly altered humanity's
ability to enjoy "right relations." With the advent of patriarchy, human
beings (specifically males) are shaped by the forces of militarism,
intolerance, oppression, sexism, slavery and violence. The origin of
patriarchal religion coincides with the origin of evil. Carol Christ, for
instance, maintains that a

> passage in Amos contains an example of the pervasive prophetic
> intolerance toward other religions that **has produced, among other
> horrors**, a climate in which witches could be put to death in
> Europe, in which the genocide of Native Americans could be
> attempted by Europeans, and in which genocide of Jews could be
> attempted by the Nazis (1987:78, emph. added).

Read unsympathetically, Carol Christ appears to say that Amos created the climate of violence which ultimately led to the Holocaust. Although Christ would probably deny any such imputation, the conclusion that the Jews are somehow responsible for the Holocaust is irresistible. As originator of patriarchy, the Hebrew Bible assumes the burden of responsibility for patriarchal evil. Amos is reproached because he produced the ideological framework for violence and intolerance; subsequent perpetrators are somewhat exonerated as mere products of this climate of violence.

Mulack argues more forcefully that patriarchal religion "becomes necessarily authoritarian." For her, "the last consequence of this process . . . presents itself in the Nazi system, which trained `German sons' to harass and kill Jewish mothers, children and fathers" (1983:248). Note, that "German sons" (how about German daughters?) were merely "trained" by a Nazi system and, hence, cannot be held fully accountable. They are presented as products of a patriarchal climate and as victims of the Nazi system. The Nazi system, on the other hand, is understood as "the last consequence" of patriarchal religion. Thus, Mulack subtly shifts the responsibility for the Holocaust from the active perpetrators of violence, the Germans, to the inventors of patriarchal religion, the Jews.

Robert Graves is refreshingly explicit about the Jewish origin of evil. He begins the last chapter of *The White Goddess*, first published in 1948, with the Nazi slogan, "the Jews are to blame for all our troubles" (1978:474). He initially rejects this "analysis" on historical grounds but later partially reinstates it, declaring that

> neither Frazer nor Hitler were far from the truth, which was that
> the early Gentile Christian borrowed from the Hebrew prophets the
> two religious concepts hitherto unknown in the West, which have
> become the prime causes of our unrest: that of a patriarchal God,
> who refuses to have any truck with Goddesses and claims to be
> self-sufficient and all-wise . . . and that of a theocratic society
> (1978:475).

These comments are quite remarkable, for Graves, in effect, blames the unrest of his time, presumably the Second World War (and the Holocaust), on the Jewish God. By locating the "prime cause" of war in Jewish patriarchal monotheism he blames the evil committed by Christians and post-Christians on "Jewish influences."

The "origin-of-patriarchy thesis" has been added to the anti-Jewish arsenal. Anti-Judaism invests Judaism with an inordinate amount of power to influence the world negatively. It suspects a Jewish spirit behind every destructive force and fears a Jewish world conspiracy. None of the scholars I have cited may be guilty of such gross anti-Jewish suspicions. Yet, the feminist paradigm of religion's Fall into patriarchy fosters anti-Jewish misrepresentations. It often singles out Hebrew monotheism as uniquely responsible for patriarchy and neglects the development of surrounding patriarchal polytheistic religions. Furthermore, it ignores two thousand years of European Christian history with its combination of Hellenistic philosophy, Roman power politics and the cultures of Central and Northern Europe all contributing to what is meant by "patriarchal monotheism."

Chapter VII

JUDAISM AS PROLOGUE

The rule of formation of prologue presents Judaism as Christianity's prehistory and conceals that it is an independent alternative tradition. The rule of formation of prologue is often found in replacement theology which identifies Judaism with the "Old Testament" and portrays it as a quaint ancestor of the church. Judaism is rendered invisible and disappears from Christian discourse with the destruction of the Temple. As Christianity's foundation it can alternately be claimed or rejected, redeemed or denounced, appropriated or repudiated.

THE END OF ISRAEL

Gerda Weiler echoes Martin Noth who claimed that in Jesus "the history of Israel had come . . . to its real end" (quoted in Klein 1978:26). In her description of deuteronomist theology Weiler maintains that God decreed Israel's final destruction. The history of Israel shows

> how this people leaves the tolerant *Weltanschauung* of its mothers, how it demonizes the penetrating love of matriarchal religion, splits off destructive aggressions and fights for dominance in the Near East with a brutal "extermination program." On the reverse side of power waits powerlessness. Israel is destroyed and ceases to exist as a state. . . .Total claim to power must lead to disaster and total destruction (1984:33).

Weiler seems unaware of the ongoing existence of Israel, ignoring the resurrection of the state of Israel after the Babylonian exile as well as in 1948. She represents Israel as if its history ended with the "Old

Testament," unrelated to any present political and religious events. Though born in Berlin in 1921, she does not associate her term "total destruction" with the Holocaust. The rule of formation of prologue impedes the awareness of the continuity of the people of Israel.

THE JUDEO-CHRISTIAN TRADITION

Most Gentiles are ignorant about Jewish culture, religion and history. The term "Judeo-Christian tradition" conceals this ignorance and enhances the suppression of Judaism as a distinct and separate religious tradition. There is no shortage of examples to argue that the term "Judeo-Christian tradition" reduces the "Judeo-" part of this idiom to the "Old Testament," effectively disguising Jewish life and theology. For instance, Dorothy Burlage refers to "Judeo-Christian influences on the female sex" (1974:96) without ever mentioning Jewish perceptions of gender. Phyllis Chesler berates the oppression of women in "Judeo-Christian Europe" (1982:99) without ever hinting at Jewish life in Christian Europe. McFague points to a "Judeo-Christian emphasis on humanity's `dominion over the earth'" (1982:178) without pursuing this biblical quote into rabbinic literature. For Moltmann-Wendel, the written records of a "Jewish-Christian faith" consist of the "Old Testament, New Testament, canon law, dogmatics" (1986:106). She neglects works of the Jewish tradition which developed independently and contemporaneously to Christianity. Minimally, the written record of a "Judeo-Christian tradition" would include the Mishnah, Talmud, the writings of Maimonides, Gersonides and the Shulkhan Aruch. Clearly, in each example, the "Judeo-" part of the tradition is equated with the Hebrew Bible and eclipsed (cf. Spretnak 1982:xv; Heine 1987:20).

In addition, the term "Judeo-Christian" occurs frequently in negative contexts where some or all of this tradition is repudiated, drawing attention to the Jewish roots of an undesirable aspect in Christianity. For instance, Daly criticizes "the myth of the Fall" through which "the Judeo-Christian tradition has been aiding and abetting the sickness of society" (1973:47; cf. McNamara 1976:145; Ruether 1983:38). However, the Fall is not a "Jewish idea," (Moltmann-Wendel's claim notwithstanding; 1977:30), but a distinctly Christian interpretation of Genesis. Jewish interpretations of Genesis understand Eve's and Adam's disobedience not as Fall and Original Sin but as the first incident of human failure to keep God's commandments. Despite numerous incidents of disobedience, humanity remains theoretically capable of keeping God's laws on earth.

To acknowledge that the "Judeo-Christian tradition" consists of two separate and independent religions can destabilize absolutist Christian truth claims. Since Judaism is always a partial disclaimer of Christianity the conflicts and disagreements between the two faiths must be concealed. The existence of a second religious identity based on the same sacred text defies triumphalist notions of God, scriptures, authority, truth, tradition, spirituality and community. The rule of formation of prologue neutralizes these competitive truth claims by disguising Israel's continued existence.

For the most part, American religious feminists have been committed to overcoming religious triumphalism and have included Jewish feminist perspectives. Most American feminist anthologies include essays by Jewish feminists and realize a basic equality between Judaism and Christianity (Christ 1979, Plaskow 1989; Ruether 1974b; Ruether and McLaughlin 1979; Kalven and Buckley 1984). Sometimes, however, the inclusion of Jewish feminists into a Christian framework allows the rule of formation of prologue to enter through the back door. One such example is *Feminist Interpretation of the Bible*, edited by Letty Russell (1985). In her concluding essay Russell poses the central question for "feminists of the Jewish and Christian faiths [who] are faced with a basic dilemma. Are they to be faithful to the teachings of the Hebrew scriptures and the Christian scriptures, or are they to be faithful to their own integrity as whole human beings?" (1985:137) Responding to this question, Russell first assumes that Jewish and Christian feminists are confronted by the same dilemma. This presupposition has been critiqued by Jewish feminists as a false universalization. The sources of Jewish women's religious oppression are not the same as those of Christian women. As Daum and McCauley point out, "it is not biblical authority, but rabbinic interpretation of male Jewish experience as embodied in halakhah that is both the starting point and the nexus of struggle for many Jewish feminists" (1983:183; cf. Umanski 1989:187-199). An uncritical Christian assumption of a shared "basic dilemma" declares the Christian experience normative, thus rendering Judaism and Jewish women's experiences invisible.

The Jewish contribution to *Feminist Interpretation of the Bible* does not respond to the question of biblical authority for Jewish feminists. Rather, Drora Setel's "Prophets and Pornography" offers a close critical reading of Hosea without reflecting hermeneutically and theologically on the meaning of Hosea's sexism for the contemporary Jewish community (1985:86-96). In contrast to the Christian contributors, who provide various hermeneutical, historical and political perspectives on the role of the Bible in Christian women's lives, Setel does not address contemporary Jewish feminist issues. Therefore, *Feminist Interpretation of the Bible* does not counter the reductionist notion that Judaism is identified with the Hebrew Bible. It fails to bring the independent Jewish interpretation of the Bible to the attention of the reader.

Another instance where Jewish feminists are rendered invisible is Delores Williams' *Sisters in the Wilderness*. Here, Jewish feminists are grouped with other white and ethnic feminists but are denied a voice distinct from Christianity or white feminism (1993:178,183). In her chapter on "Womanist-Feminist Dialogue: Differences and Commonalities," Williams mentions Jewish feminists in a list of different ethnic feminists without quoting any particular author. While the index refers to Hispanic, Native American and Asian feminists, Jewish feminists are not listed. Likewise, in her textual exegesis of Hagar, Williams depends on Christian exegetes such as Roland De Vaux and Gerhart von Rad but ignores traditional Jewish and unconventional Jewish feminist voices (e.g. Teubal 1984, 1990; Fuchs 1985). Their voices become doubly invisible: traditional Jewish interpretations of the Hebrew Bible are overlooked because Christianity supersedes Judaism and has rendered its reading obsolete. Jewish feminist interpretations are neglected because they are fused with white feminism and rejected as racist.

INCLUSION AND APPROPRIATION

The rule of formation of prologue encourages the dispossession of Judaism. Some Christian theologians appropriate and incorporate Jewish theological concepts into Christianity. The "Jewishness" of these notions receives little acknowledgement and does not change the overall negative assessment of Jewish patriarchy. Positive elements of Judaism are expropriated. Christa Mulack, for example, uses cabalistic thought as the foundation of her Christian feminist reformation without further reflecting the legitimacy of her use and inclusion of a different tradition. In her introduction to *Die Weiblichkeit Gottes* she merely states that

this God imagery was taken from Jewish mysticism, the cabala, which shall serve as an exemplary foundation. It appears to be particularly helpful for this analysis because of its following characteristics:
1. In its current form it was formulated exclusively by men.
2. It is based on biblical statements about God.
3. It is accepted by both Jewish and Christian mystics.
4. It does not depict God as exclusively male (1983:9).

Mulack does not reflect on the implications of the fact that the cabala was not merely written by "men," but by Jewish men whose marginalization and oppression in Christian Europe might have influenced their thinking. Mulack's positive evaluation of cabalistic female God language is disconnected from her overall negative assessment of Judaism. This incorporation of Judaism as "exemplary foundation" into her Christian feminist reconstruction, without any revision of her negative judgment of Judaism, constitutes a dispossession. As Thistlethwaite has argued for the inclusion of Black women's literature into white feminist theology, unself-conscious inclusion of Jewish (or Black) thought into the dominant Christian (or white) discourse fails to safeguard the integrity and difference of the minority experience. Thistlethwaite has warned against the uncritical use of Black women's writings and maintains that "as a white feminist, I cannot use the fiction of Black women as a source in the same way I have been able to use the fiction of white women as a resource for white feminist theology. In approaching the literature of Black women I must be aware of difference" (1989:4). Similarly, Christian feminists must beware of the appropriation and reinterpretation of Jewish texts and of approaching Judaism as prologue and resource of Christianity.

Virginia Mollenkott incorporates the concept of God's *Shekhinah* into her interpretation of the New Testament. The notion of the *Shekhinah* as God's immanent and relational presence among the people of Israel assumed importance after the destruction of the Temple. The *Shekhinah* is therefore a primarily post New Testament Jewish idea. Based on Patai, Mollenkott admits that "the word Shekinah does not appear in the Bible, but the concept certainly does" (1983:40). She then traces the concept of the *Shekhinah* through the Hebrew Bible and concludes:

> The Shekinah glory of God, that "feminine" Presence, dwelt in the temple of Jerusalem; but John 1:14 together with John 2:21 asserts that the body of Christ has now become the temple and is the perfect dwelling place of the Shekinah glory. . . . In other words the presence of Christ the Shekinah within the worshiping

> congregation, is expected to expose the absurdity of all classist,
> racist, or sexist prejudices (1983:40).

Mollenkott does not honor and respect the *Shekhinah* as a genuine development of Jewish God symbolism and a Jewish embodiment of feminist qualities of relationality, immanence and femininity. Rather, she appropriates it for Christianity. Her claim that the "body of Christ . . . is the perfect dwelling place" for the *Shekhinah* reasserts traditional replacement theology and dispossesses a Jewish concept for Christian purposes. It fails to preserve the Jewish interpretation of the *Shekhinah* in its integrity and distinctiveness.

FEMINIST UNIVERSALISM

Feminist insistence on women's universal experience has been critiqued by a variety of women for its class, race and religious limitations (cf. chapter 1). The claim that women are primarily oppressed by sexism has been exposed as a false universalization of white Christian middle class experience which negates the experiences of Jewish, Black and poor women. The stipulation that all women accept sexism the fundamental form of oppression renders the experience of "other" minority women invisible and expects them to give up allegiance with their communities. Mary Daly's critique of religion is a case in point. She dismisses all religious and secular communities because they are

> infrastructures of the edifice of patriarchy. All are erected as parts
> of the male's shelter against anomie. Consequently, women are the
> objects of male terror, the projected personification of "the
> Enemy," the real objects under attack in all the wars of patriarchy
> (1978:39).

Daly does not distinguish between dominant and marginal religious traditions but argues forcefully that "the real objects under attack" are women. She dismisses and minimizes other structures of domination to the point of denial and disregards the empowering role of religion for oppressed communities. In her discussion of the Holocaust she subsumes antisemitism under sexism as the ultimate context of oppression. The "roots of the evil of genocide," according to her, are not found

in the kind of research which shrinks/localizes perspectives on
oppression so that they can be contained strictly within ethnic and
"religious group" dimensions. The sado-rituals of patriarchy are
perpetually perpetrated. The plane/domain is the entire planet. The
paradigm and context for genocide is trite, everyday banalized
gynocide (1978:311).

The Holocaust as a unique incident of genocide in the 20th
century is denied and universalized into an event which is "perpetrated
perpetually" and on "the entire planet." She denounces the analysis of
antisemitism and understands research on the Holocaust as reactionary
adherence to a "shrunken and localized perspective." Universalism
becomes an instrument to deny the existence of antisemitism as well
as the experience of Jewish women and men who have suffered and
continue to suffer from antisemitism.

As I have argued in chapter 1, most women experience sexism
in conjunction with other forms of oppression. For Jewish women,
sexism is often colored by antisemitism while antisemitism is
amplified by sexism. Oftentimes, the two cannot be distinguished, as,
for instance, in "JAP" jokes. The stereotype of the "Jewish American
Princess," which continues to be popular on university campuses,
illustrates the collusion of sexism and antisemitism. The victim is
attacked both as female and Jew. Whether one calls "JAP" jokes
primarily sexist or antisemitic is a matter of choice. It might depend
on the individual who uses the jokes. The feminist analysis of sexism
illuminates one segment of Jewish women's experience of oppression.
But without an analysis of antisemitism it will remain incomplete.

The radical feminist call for solidarity of all women across the
boundaries of class, religion, race, sexual preference and nationality
sounds not unlike traditional calls for conversion. Daly's vision of a
cosmic sisterhood discourages women's allegiances with Jewish, Black
and Third World men in the struggle against antisemitism, racism and
imperialism. It is reminiscent of the universal primacy of class in
Marxism which declared the "woman question" and the "Jewish
question" *Nebenwidersprüche* [secondary conflicts]. It is also
reminiscent of Christian ideals of a universal, catholic community
which rejects Jewish particularity.

Wilson-Kastner promotes a more traditional Christian universalism which understands the resurrection of Christ as "triumph for all
humanity, indeed for all the world, over the forces of alienation."

The cosmic vision of feminism is not an illusory dream of naive individuals, but in its most thoroughgoing and radical form is the vision of the gospel, the promise made by God to the world through Jesus Christ. The struggles of feminism find their fullest context and their strongest promise of fulfillment in the risen Christ (1983:114).

Wilson-Kastner's feminist universalism denies Jewish particularity. She expects Jewish women to join the new, superior, universal community. Her reformist feminist stance joins hands with the radical post--Christian thinking of Daly: leave the particular and join the universal feminist community. Daly's radical post-Christian "sisterhood as cosmic church" (1973:155) which later evolved into the equally controversial "Race of Women" (Daly 1985b:4) echoes Wilson-Kastner's triumphalist Christian universalism. So does, to a certain extent, Schüssler Fiorenza's "discipleship of equals." Her explanation that "the Christians affirmed at their baptism that the Christian call eliminates all distinctions of religion, race, class and caste and leads into a truly universal and catholic community of disciples" (1979a:141) contains similar universalist expectations.

At the heart of the Christian persecution of the synagogue was the Jewish assertion of a separate identity. Christian theology has not been able to accept this "stiff necked, stubborn and blind" people who insisted on being different although the church held out the option of conversion. Jews have resisted conversion to Christianity as they have declined modernity's bourgeois and socialist invitations to assimilate. Jews have resisted Christian and post-Christian expectation to break "through all limitations of religion, class, race, and gender" (Fiorenza 1979a:140) and have insisted on separateness.

Anti-Judaism in Christian and Christian-rooted feminist theology manifests itself when the Jewish "No" cannot be accepted theologically, when the difference between Christianity and Judaism cannot be affirmed and when Jewish particularity cannot be honored as a positive and constructive contribution to feminist theology. The rule of formation of prologue originates in the Christian inability to accept Judaism as a different and equal religious alternative. Audre Lorde has pointed out that patriarchy developed three ways of dealing with difference, namely to "ignore it," "copy it" or "destroy it" (1984:115). The rule of formation of prologue corresponds to these patterns: it "ignores" Judaism in terms such as "Judeo-Christian tradition," which presuppose that Judaism has ceased to exist; it "copies," appropriates and assimilates Jewish concepts deemed feminist and positive; finally, it "destroys" and dissolves particularity and difference of minority experiences in its vision of a universal, egalitarian community .

Chapter VIII

THE TEACHING OF RESPECT

I have argued that Christian theology incorporates an anti-Jewish myth which renders Judaism the antithesis, scapegoat and prologue of Christianity. This teaching of contempt supports an objective system of oppressions because it reinforces Gentile perceptions of Judaism as inferior, evil and Other. Anti-Judaism can exist without the intention of individual authors and without the presence of personal prejudice. Charlotte Klein's remarks are confirmed by my observations:

> The expressions "hatred" and "contempt" are certainly too strong. . . . The [Christian] authors deliberately avoid anything of the kind. But judgements without adequate knowledge of the facts, an excessive trust in their predecessors in the field of Jewish studies, disregard, a certain want of empathy such as is often exhibited today towards other non-Christian religions: enough of all this is found in the authors whose opinions are examined here. And the same tendencies will certainly be roused and strengthened in most of the uncritical readers (1978:10-11).

My study has focused on the representation of Judaism in feminist religious writings. In collecting and interpreting often casual and unintentional descriptions of Judaism I have found that some feminist theologians depict Judaism as the antithesis of feminist values and identify it excessively with patriarchy and sexism. The cumulative effect of these accounts renders Judaism inferior to Christianity and paganism.

In addition, the writings I have analyzed emphasize the responsibility of Judaism for the origin of patriarchal religion. The Jewish God and Hebrew scriptures are singled out and depicted as the cause of militarism, intolerance, authoritarianism and sexism. The Jewish roots of Christianity are blamed for sexism in the church. The Jewish scapegoat diverts ethical responsibility from the actual instigators of Christian patriarchy as it triumphed in Western civilization.

Lastly, I have argued that Judaism disappears from Christian consciousness as a viable and inviolate religious alternative after the rise of Christianity. Instead, Judaism is seen as an extension of Christianity whose feminist features can be incorporated and dispossessed. Jewish particularity is denied and superseded by a universal Christian or post-Christian feminist vision.

The presence of the anti-Jewish myth in some Christian and neo-pagan feminist writings does not imply that feminist theology is irredeemably anti-Jewish. For each of the stereotypes I documented, I could have cited sources which manage to avoid this anti-Jewish pattern. Sometimes, the same author who incorporated one particular stereotype succeeded in sidestepping another. What, then, explains the recurrence of the anti-Jewish myth in feminist religious writings and what can be done to avoid it?

The awareness of a powerful and pervasive anti-Judaism is a first step toward overcoming it. Knowledge of the history, form and function of anti-Judaism enables theologians who unconsciously participate in this cultural and religious tradition to extricate themselves from it. In order to institute such awareness, the history of Christian antisemitism and the theology of anti-Judaism must become part of any theological education as well as of feminist consciousness. The discussions and articles on feminist anti-Judaism which have been published during the last ten years have succeeded in making Christian and Goddess feminists more sensitive to the issue. Consider the following example from *In Our Mother's Garden*:

> For some time, Chinese women have taken comfort in knowing that Jesus advocated equality of the sexes, in spite of the Jewish patriarchal custom, and that Paul's teachings on women were limited by the cultural conditions of his time. But today, Jewish feminists caution us against anti-Semitic prejudices, and feminist biblical scholars argue that Paul's' bias against women took place in a much wider process of patriarchalization of the early church (Pui-Lan 1988:26).

Kwok Pui-Lan reiterates the antithetical arguments of the "feminist Jesus versus Jewish patriarchy" and "Paul's Jewish cultural conditioning," but then qualifies them with an awareness of anti-Judaism. She does not elaborate and leaves the reader to decide whether to interpret her original statements as true or false. Nevertheless, the insertion directs the reader's attention to the problem of antisemitism and constitutes a helpful first step.

The recognition of the anti-Jewish heritage in Christian thought should lead to a profound change in theological reasoning. Despite a general awareness of anti-Judaism, few theologians are willing to institute radical change. Instead, responses to anti-Judaism sometimes remain on the surface and are content with linguistic and cosmetic adjustments. This does not surprise because the weight of anti-Judaism is usually underestimated. Let me point out four avoidance strategies that lead to a misjudgment of the pervasiveness of the anti-Jewish myth: trivialization, particularization, spiritualization and universalization (cf. Daly 1973:5).

Anti-Judaism is *trivialized* by comparing it to seemingly more urgent problems, such as racism, poverty, genocide or the environment. Sometimes, attempts to raise the issue of antisemitism are blocked by referring to the greater need to attend to other oppressions. Jews, one is told, are white, affluent, powerful and in no imminent danger. Hence, antisemitism is not a serious topic. In *The Wrath of Jonah*, Rosemary and Herman Ruether dismiss Jewish fears as belonging "more to the realm of Jewish subjective feelings than to objective realities. . . . Jews in the Diaspora, especially in North America, enjoy unparalleled power, prosperity, and acceptance. The Christian world, by and large, has come to identify with their rights, not only to exist, but to prosper as a religious and ethnic group" (1989:224). Having trivialized antisemitism into the realm of subjective emotion, the Ruethers feel free to make their case against Israel and to indict Zionism as an ideology that was "bred in the sick world of Western anti-Semitism, racial nationalism, and imperialist colonialism in the Middle East" (1989:221). The trivialization allows customary negative evaluations of Judaism to continue.

Another strategy of avoidance is to *particularize* anti-Judaism, reducing it to somebody else's problem. In this case, antisemitism is dismissed as a "German problem," a "Black problem," a "neo-pagan problem" or a "right-wing problem." However, as I have tried to show, the anti-Jewish discourse of Christian theology has infiltrated all Christian and post-Christian world views. By particularizing the problem one is pushing it into somebody else's backyard in order to avoid confronting its existence in one's own thinking.

A third avoidance strategy is the *spiritualization* of the problem. Jews are condemned, so the argument goes, on religious grounds only and theological statements about the Pharisees or ancient

Israelites have nothing to do with attitudes towards contemporary Jews. It is quite possible, so the argument continues, to denounce Jews theologically without being biased against the actual Jewish community. Such a position, however, cannot account for the persistence of antisemitism through the ages. If, indeed, it were possible to maintain theological images of the "evil Jew" without affecting the people, violence against Jews would have stopped a long time ago.

Lastly, anti-Judaism can be *universalized*. A universal concern for injustice, inhumanity and cruelty can be a strategy to deflect attention from antisemitism. Rosemary and Herman Ruether's argument that "concern about Jewish suffering" must be grounded in "concern for all human suffering" is a case in point. They write: "To be concerned about Jewish suffering obliges one to be concerned about black South African suffering, women's suffering, the suffering of the homeless refugee people in many parts of the world, and Palestinian suffering" (1989:218). Attention is moved away from the Jews to other groups of people. The result is that "Jewish suffering" is treated as a political metaphor without caring for the Jewish people. In Germany, for example, some people apply the lessons of the Holocaust to Turks and foreigners as "the Jews of today." Instead of a thorough examination of the specific contours and history of German Christian anti-Judaism, they transfer their compassion to anyone but the Jews. A universal concern for human suffering can serve to divert from the seriousness of the anti-Jewish myth.

Each of these strategies deflects from a sincere discussion of anti-Judaism. After the Holocaust, however, antisemitism can no longer be dismissed as a minor prejudice among the ignorant few. Anti-Judaism is not a relic of an ancient past, overcome by enlightenment and goodwill, but continues to be a formidable force in the modern world. It is reestablishing itself in the political arenas of many European countries, not to mention the Middle East.

In order to counter the teaching of contempt we need more than verbal condemnations and well-intentioned dialogues. Half-hearted attempts at education will not be able to confront antisemitism effectively because it is a political and religious force that affects more than the rational mind. We must also understand the affective basis of antisemitism, the emotional passion which accompanies stereotypes and ideologies. Deborah Lipstadt warns in *Denying the Holocaust*:

> Reasoned dialogue has a limited ability to withstand an assault by
> the mythic power of falsehood, especially when that falsehood is
> rooted in an age-old social and cultural phenomenon. There was no
> rational basis for the Nazi atrocities. . . . Mythical thinking and the
> force of the irrational have a strange and compelling allure for the
> educated and uneducated alike (1993:25).

Antisemitism has always had the uncanny ability to mobilize
and unite opposing social groups and to serve as glue between rich
and poor, educated and uneducated, left and right. It taps into feelings
of discontent and resentment, and directs them towards a socially
approved target. Liberal forms of enlightenment and dialogue alone do
not have the power to address these emotional issues. Instead, we have
to understand antisemitism as a religious symbol system which "does
not depend on rational assent, for a symbol also functions on levels of
the psyche other than the rational. Religion fulfills deep psychic needs
by providing symbols and rituals that enable people to cope with crisis
situations" (Christ 1987:118). The emergence of women's consciousness was such a crisis situation. In forging new religious identities
feminists reached back into familiar thought patterns, thereby unself-
consciously adopting anti-Judaism and integrating it into feminist
theological discourse.

As Carol Christ has pointed out, symbol systems cannot simply
be rejected, "they must be replaced. Where there is no replacement,
the mind will revert to familiar structures at times of crisis, bafflement
or defeat" (1987:118). Anti-Judaism is such a symbol system which
has, at times, been rejected but has always reemerged in times of
crisis. It is therefore critical to move beyond mere rejection of
antisemitism. Instead, we must *replace* the teaching of contempt with
a "teaching of respect" (Williamson 1993:245).

The teaching of respect foils the rules of formation of antithesis,
scapegoat and prologue. It challenges the reader on intellectual as well
as emotional levels because it demands a shift from the traditional
feeling of contempt to the unfamiliar attitude of respect. The long
history of Jewish symbolization as evil must be substituted with a
teaching of acclaim and commendation.

Specifically, the teaching of respect acknowledges the Jewish
roots of feminist elements in the Christian message. It presents the
Jewish tradition of monotheism (God), community (Israel) and practice
(Torah) in its distinctiveness and integrity. The teaching of respect
makes an effort to describe Judaism in such a manner that a
Jewish-identified feminist can assent. It holds Jewish women's "No"

to Christian superiority and conversion attempts in esteem. It explains the peculiar mechanisms of Jewish oppression and alerts the reader to the history of Christian violence against Jews. The teaching of respect values Jewish contributions to the struggle against oppressions based on gender, race and class, pointing out that Jews have often extended their commitment to prophetic justice to include other groups. A teaching of respect emphasizes that Jewish women have made gains (or lost ground) in their own communities at about the same time and the same rate as their sisters of the majority religions, whether in Rome, Alexandria, Cordoba, Baghdad, Prague, Berlin or New York. The teaching of respect confirms that Jews have contributed to the common good of their cultures in and through their distinct and particular communities.

The teaching of respect is not equivalent to uncritical philo-Semitism and a romantic idealization of Jews and Judaism. Rather, it calls for a "theological theory of Jews and Judaism in which Jews can recognize themselves" (Williamson 1993:245). It is not a rule of unconditional approval but remains committed to and vigilant for the well-being of this religious minority. It maintains an element of admiration even in periods of disagreement. Above all, it is suspicious of the impulse to criticize Jews and Judaism. Any criticism of Judaism must be reflected in the context of century-old Jew-hatred and must account for its own place in that history: does it reinforce the tradition of Jew-hating or does it break with it? By way of analogy, we may look at legitimate criticisms of feminist theology. An author who has no vested interest in the survival and flourishing of feminist theology and launches into criticizing it needs to be questioned as to his or her motivation. Since feminists and Jews are beleaguered minorities, attacks from the powerful (patriarchal, Gentile-Christian) majorities are usually intended to negate our communities. Criticism can only be accepted as legitimate and helpful, if there is a commitment to the survival of our communities, and if attention is given to the structures of oppression which deny our well-being.

> Those who offer criticisms of a group that has been the target of racism for long periods in history must carefully and systematically show that they are aware of the dangers of playing into the history of racism, that they are consciously aware of how that racism functions, and that they are taking systematic steps in all their statements and writings simultaneously to confront and disavow that racism or anti-Semitism even as they make their specific and limited criticism (M. Lerner 1992:99).

Criticisms are not necessarily signs of disrespect. On the contrary, they are an integral part of any respectful relation. Respectful criticism presupposes the existence of relationship, a precondition often not met by those who criticize Judaism. To this day, Christian theologians fault Judaism for a variety of theological and ethical shortcomings, complaints not made for the benefit of Jews and Judaism but for the self-aggrandizement of Christians. The negative feminist assessment analyzed in this book occurred almost always as an aside, a marginal remark. These remarks were not intended as constructive criticism of Judaism but were uttered in pursuit of other theological agendas. They did not happen in a relational context and were not designed to constructively change Judaism. The work of Jewish feminists, though also profoundly critical of Judaism, is usually not anti-Jewish. Jewish feminists are not distinguished from non-Jewish feminists by the severity of their denunciation of patriarchy but by their willingness to allow for reinterpretation and change within the tradition. Anti-Judaism means the rejection of Judaism and the refusal to enter into relationship with an evolving and dynamic community. Legitimate criticism of Judaism is concerned with the continuing vitality of the Jewish faith community through radical disagreement and empathy, dispute and respect.

To some extent, this relational quality of legitimate criticism cuts across the distinction of Jew and Gentile. Some Jews have internalized antisemitism, feel contempt for Judaism and have severed their ties to the community. Since antisemitism, as any other form of oppression, can be internalized, Jews are not automatically exempt from the responsibility to be fair and respectful in their criticism. Michael Lerner challenges Jews to "ask themselves the following question: What have I done in the past year to show that I am lovingly committed to Judaism or the Jewish people, apart from engaging in acts of criticism of Israel or the Jews?" (1992:104). Like him, I would make "a strong and loving connection" the prerequisite to distinguish criticism from potential anti-Judaism. Legitimate criticism is well-balanced, mindful of the context, limited in scope, not selective and willing to engage in dialogue. It maintains a basic level of respect and explicitly resists being used to justify hatred and injustice.

I found that the cultural and theological differences between feminist theologians assumed secondary importance with respect to the teaching of contempt. Anti-Judaism unites Christian and neo-pagan, German and American, progressive and conservative feminist theologians. Anti-Judaism is a Christian theological formation which transcends national, gender, race and time boundaries.

But there are differences in degree: although the rules of formation of the anti-Jewish myth can be ascertained in both West German and US American feminist writings, the German books surveyed incorporated stronger anti-Jewish language and imagery than their American counterparts even when the particular argument was the same. This can be explained by the peculiar history of German anti-Judaism which is shaped by Lutheran antithetical theological constructions, a specific type of historical critical scholarship, the legacy of antisemitic ideology of the 19th century and, above all, the Holocaust. German feminist theologians work without the benefits of a vibrant Jewish community and repeat anti-Jewish motifs without being challenged. Some of those mentioned in this study revised their arguments after they had been challenged (Weiler 1989); others steadfastly insisted on the rectitude of their arguments (cf. Heschel 1993). American feminists, in contrast, generally accepted Jewish criticism with greater openness and were more willing to respond to Jewish criticisms in a constructive way.

Feminist communities must begin to replace the teaching of contempt with a teaching of appreciation which explicitly affirms the legitimacy and vitality of the Jewish tradition. Because of the peculiar nature of this myth, its religious roots and emotional appeal, feminists must move beyond verbal condemnations and cosmetic changes towards genuine respect for Judaism.

BIBLIOGRAPHY

Adler, Margot. 1979. *Drawing Down the Moon*. Boston: Beacon Press.

Allport, Gordon. [1954] 1985. *The Nature of Prejudice*. Reading, MA: Addison-Wesley Publishing Company.

Andolsen, Barbara. 1986. *Daughters of Jefferson, Daughters of Bootblacks*. Macon, GA: Mercer University Press.

Atkinson, Clarissa, Constance Buchanan and Margaret Miles, eds. 1985. *Immaculate and Powerful: The Female in Sacred and Social Reality*. Boston: Beacon Press.

Austen, Ralph A. 1994. "The Uncomfortable Relationship: African Enslavement in the Common History of Blacks and Jews." *Tikkun* 2 (March/April) 9:65-68.

Baader, Maria. 1993. "Zum Abschied." In *Entfernte Verbindungen. See* Hügel 1993.

Bachofen, Johann Jakob. [1861] 1967. *Myth, Religion and Motherright*. Translated by Ralph Manheim. New Jersey: Princeton University Press.

Bailey, Randall C. 1991. "Beyond Identification: The Use of Africans in Old Testament Poetry and Narratives." In *Stony the Road We Trod. See* Felder 1991.

Balch, David. 1981. *Let Wives be Submissive: The Domestic Code in 1 Peter*. Chico, CA: Scholars Press.

Baron, Salo Wittmayer. 1969. *A Social and Religious History of the Jews*. Vol. 13. New York: Columbia University Press.

Barr, James. 1988. "Abba isn't Daddy." *Journal of Theological Studies* 39 (April):28-47.

Barstow, Anne Llewellyn. 1994. *Witchcraze: A New History of the European Witch Hunts*. San Francisco: Harper and Collins.

Barth, Markus. 1968. "Was Paul an Anti-Semite?" *Journal of Ecumenical Studies* 5:78-104.

---. 1977. "Das Volk Gottes. Juden und Christen in der Botschaft des Paulus." In *Paulus, Apostat oder Apostel? Jüdische und christliche Antworten*. Edited by Markus Barth. Regensburg: Pustet.

Barz, Monika, Hertha Leistner and Ute Wild, eds. 1987. *Hättest Du gedacht, daß wir so viele sind?* Stuttgart: Kreuz Verlag.

Bauer, Yehuda. 1982. *History of the Holocaust*. New York: Franklin Watts.

Baum, Gregory. [1960] 1965. *Is the New Testament Anti-Semitic?* rev. ed. New York: Paulist Press.

Beck, Evelyn Torton, ed. 1982. *Nice Jewish Girls*. Trumansburg, NY: The Crossing Press.

Beck, Norman. 1985. *Mature Christianity*. Selinsgrove: Susquehanna University Press.

Bernal, Martin. 1987, 1991. *Black Athena: The Afroasiatic Roots of Classical Civilization*. Vol. 1 and 2. New Brunswick: Rutgers University Press.

Biale, Rachel. 1984. *Women and Jewish Law*. New York: Schocken Books.

Binford, Sallie. 1982. "Myths and Matriarchies." In *The Politics of Women's Spirituality. See* Spretnak 1982.

Bitton-Jackson, Livia. 1982. *Madonna or Courtesan: The Jewish Woman in Christian Literature*. New York: Seabury Press.

Blanke, H., L. Napholcz, et.al., eds. 1986. *Dokumentation zum Konflikt um Küng, Wissenschaftsfreiheit und lesbische Liebe*. Tübingen.

Blenkinsopp, Joseph. 1980. "Tanakh and New Testament: A Christian Perspective." In *Biblical Studies: Meeting Ground of Jews and Christian*. Edited by Helga Croner, Leon Klenicki and Lawrence Boadt CSP. New York: Paulist Press.

Boneh, Nahum (Mular). 1977. *The Holocaust and the Revolt*. Offprint from the Book *Pinsk*. Vol 1. Part 2. Translated from the Hebrew by G. Eliasberg. Tel Aviv.

Borowitz, Eugene. 1980. *Contemporary Christologies: A Jewish Response*. New York: Paulist.

Boyarin, Daniel. 1993. *Carnal Israel: Reading Sex in Talmudic Culture*. Berkeley, CA: University of California Press.

Brandon, Samuel G. F. 1968. *The Trial of Jesus of Nazareth*. New York: Stein and Day.

Bratton, Fred Glaston. 1969. *The Crime of Christendom: The Theological Sources of Christian Anti-Semitism*. Boston: Beacon Press.

Bridenthal, Renate, Atina Grossmann and Marion Kaplan, eds. 1984. *When Biology Became Destiny*. New York: Monthly Review Press.

Briggs, Sheila. 1985. "Images of Women and Jews in Nineteenth and Twentieth Century Theology." In *Immaculate and Powerful*. See Atkinson 1985.

Bright, John. 1975. *History of Israel*. Philadelphia: Westminster Press.

Brock, Rita Nakashima. 1988. *Journeys by Heart: A Christology of Erotic Power*. New York: Crossroad.

Brockmann, Doris. 1987. "Die Weiblichkeit Gottes: Zu Christa Mulacks Programmatik der Neubestimmung des Göttlichen." In *Der Gott der Männer und die Frauen*. See Wacker 1987a.

Brooten, Bernadette. 1982a. "Jüdinnen zur Zeit Jesu." In *Frauen in der Männerkirche*. Edited by Bernadette Brooten and Norbert Greinacher. Munich: Kaiser Verlag. Translated into German by Marcus Lefebure from *Concilium: Women in a Men's Church*. Vol 136. Edited by Virgil Elizondo and Norbert Greinacher. New York: Seabury Press. 1980.

---. 1982b. "Konnten Frauen im alten Judentum die Scheidung betreiben?" *Evangelische Theologie* 42 (1):66-80.

---. 1982c. *Women Leaders in the Ancient Synagogue*. Chico, CA: Scholars Press.

---. 1985. "Early Christian Women and Their Cultural Context: Issues of Method in Historical Reconstruction." In *Feminist Perspectives on Biblical Scholarship*. See A. Y. Collins 1985.

---. 1986. "Jewish Women's History in the Roman Period: A Task for Christian Theology." In *Christians Among Jews and Gentiles*. Edited by George Nickelsburg. Philadelphia: Fortress Press.

Brown, Barbara Zikmund. 1987. "The Trinity and Women's Experience." *The Christian Century* (April 15):354-357.

Brownmiller, Susan. 1975. *Against Our Will*. New York: Bantam Books.

Brumlik, Micha. 1985. "Alt, Rinser, Jung, u.a.: Über den neuen christlichen Antijudaismus." *links* 181 (April):35-37.

---. 1986. "Die Angst vor dem Vater: Judenfeindliche Tendenzen im Umkreis neuer sozialer Bewegungen." In *Antisemitismus nach dem Holocaust*. Edited by Alphons Silbermann and Julius Schoeps. Cologne: Verlag Wissenschaft und Politik.

Budapest, Z. 1980. "Readers' Response." *Christian Century* (November 26):1162-1163.

Bulkien, Elly, Minnie Bruce Pratt and Barbara Smith, eds. 1984. *Yours In Struggle*. New York: Long Haul Press.

Burlage, Dorothe. 1974. "Judeo-Christian Influences on Female Sexuality." In *Sexist Religion and Women in the Church: No More Silence*. Edited by Alice Hagemann. New York: Association Press.

Cady, Susan, Marian Ronan and Hal Taussig. 1986. *Sophia: The Future of Feminist Spirituality*. San Francisco: Harper & Row Publishers.

Cannon, Katie Geneva. 1988. *Black Womanist Ethics*. Atlanta, GA: Scholars Press.

Carmody, Denise Lardner. 1982. *Feminism and Christianity*. Nashville: Abingdon.

---. 1988. *Biblical Woman*. New York: Crossroad Publishing Company.

Carrol, Elisabeth. 1982. "Kann die Herrschaft der Männer gebrochen werden?" In *Frauen in der Männerkirche*. *See* Brooten 1982a.

Chesler, Phyllis. 1982. "The Amazon Legend." In *The Politics of Women's Spirituality*. *See* Spretnak 1982.

Chicago, Judy. 1982. "Our Heritage is our Power." In *The Politics of Women's Spirituality*. *See* Spretnak 1982.

Christ, Carol. 1979. "Why Women Need the Goddess." In *Womanspirit Rising*. Edited by Carol Christ and Judith Plaskow. San Francisco: Harper & Row Publishers.

---. 1980. *Diving Deep and Surfacing*. Boston: Beacon Press.

---. 1985. "Symbols of Goddess and God in Feminist Theology." In *The Book of the Goddess*. *See* Olson 1985.

---. 1987. *Laughter of Aphrodite*. San Francisco: Harper & Row Publishers.

Cohen, Jeremy. 1982. *The Friars and the Jews*. Ithaca, NY: Cornell University Press.

Cohn, Haim. 1967. *The Trial and Death of Jesus*. New York: Harper & Row Publishers.

Collins, Adela Yarbro, ed. 1985. *Feminist Perspectives on Biblical Scholarship*. Chico, CA: Scholars Press.

Collins, Sheila. 1974. *A Different Heaven and Earth*. Valley Forge, PA: Judson Press.

---. 1979. "Reflections on the Meaning of Herstory." In *Womanspirit Rising*. *See* Christ 1979.

---. 1982. "The Personal Is Political." In *The Politics of Women's Spirituality. See* Spretnak 1982.

Cook, Michael. 1978. "Jesus and the Pharisees--The Problem as it Stands Today." *Journal of Ecumenical Studies* 15:441-460.

Copher, Charles C. 1991. "The Black Presence in the Old Testament." In *Stony the Road We Trod. See* Felder 1991.

Croner, Helga, ed. 1977. *Stepping Stones to Further Jewish-Christian Relations.* New York: Paulist Press.

Culpepper, Emily. 1987. "Philosophia: Feminist Methodology for Constructing a Female Train of Thought." *Journal of Feminist Studies in Religion* 3 (2):8-16.

Daly, Mary. 1973. *Beyond God the Father*. Boston: Beacon Press.

---. 1978. *Gyn/Ecology*. Boston: Beacon Press.

---. [1968] 1985a. *The Church And The Second Sex: With a Feminist Postchristian Introduction and Archaic Afterwords by the Author*. Boston: Beacon Press.

---. 1985b. *Pure Lust*. Boston: Beacon Press

Daum, Annette. 1982. "Blaming the Jews for the Death of the Goddess." In *Nice Jewish Girls. See* E. T. Beck 1982. First published *Lilith* (1979) 7:12-13.

---. 1984. "A Jewish Feminist View." *Theology Today* 41:294-300.

Daum, Annette and Deborah McCauley. 1983. "Jewish-Christian Feminist Dialogue: A Wholistic Vision." *Union Seminary Quarterly Review* 38 (2):147-189.

Davies, Alan. 1979. "On Religious Myths and Their Secular Translation: Some Historical Reflections." In *AntiSemitism and the Foundations of Christianity*. Edited by Alan Davies. New York: Paulist Press.

Davies, Steve. 1985. "The Canaanite-Hebrew Goddess." In *The Book of the Goddess. See* Olson 1985.

Davis, Elizabeth Gould. 1971. *The First Sex*. Baltimore: G.P. Putnam & Sons.

De Beauvoir, Simone. [1952] 1974. *The Second Sex*. Translated by H.M.Parshley. New York: Vintage Books.

Decke, Bettina. 1987. "Antijudaismus im neuen Gewand: Exkurs über feministisch christlichen Fundamentalismus." *tageszeitung* (November 31):16-18.

---. 1988. "Christlicher Antijudaismus und Feminismus." In *Der sogenannte Gott*. Edited by Albert Sellner. Frankfurt: Scarabäus.

De Croy, Merode. 1982. "Die Rolle der Frau im Alten Testament." In *Frauen in der Männerkirche. See* Brooten 1982.

Downing, Christine. 1984. *The Goddess.* New York: Crossroad Publishing Company.

Dworkin, Andrea. 1983. *Right Wing Women.* New York: Coward-McCann.

Eckardt, A. Roy. 1967. *Elder and Younger Brothers.* New York: Schocken Books.

———. 1974. *Your People, My People.* New York: Quadrangle Books.

———. 1989. *Black, Woman, Jew.* Bloomington: Indiana University Press.

Eckardt A. Roy and Alice Eckardt. 1988. *Long Night's Journey Into Day.* Detroit: Wayne State University Press.

Efroymson, David P. 1979. "The Patristic Connection." In *AntiSemitism and the Foundations of Christianity. See* Davies 1979.

Elshtain, Jean Behtke. 1981. *Public Man, Private Woman.* Princeton: Princeton University Press.

Engels, Friedrich. [1848] 1970. *The Origin of The Family, Private Property and the State.* With an Introduction and Notes by Eleanor Burke Leacock. New York: International Publishers Company.

Ericksen, Robert. 1985. *Theologians Under Hitler.* New Haven: Yale University Press.

Fanon, Frantz. 1967. *Black Skin White Masks.* Translated by Charles Lam Markman. New York: Grove Press.

Farley, Margaret. 1976. "Sources of Sexual Inequality in the History of Christian Thought." *The Journal of Religion* 56 (April):162-176.

Felder, Cain Hope. 1991. "Race, Racism and the Biblical Narrative." In *Stony the Road We Trod.* Edited by Felder. Minneapolis: Fortress Press.

Finkelstein, Louis. 1972. *Phariseeism in the Making.* New York: Ktav Books.

Fiorenza, Elisabeth Schüssler. 1978. "Women in the Pre-Pauline and Pauline Churches." *Union Seminary Quarterly Review* 33 (Spring/Summer):153-166.

———. 1979a. "Women in the Early Christian Movement." In *Womanspirit Rising. See* Christ 1979.

———. 1979b. "Word, Spirit and Power: Women in Early Christian Communities." In *Women of Spirit.* Edited by Ruether.

---. 1980. "Der Beitrag der Frau zur urchristlichen Bewegung. Kritische Über-legungen zur Rekonstruktion urchristlicher Geschichte." In *Traditionen der Befreiung*. Edited by Willi Schottroff und Wolfgang Stegemann. Munich: Kaiser Verlag.

---. 1983. *In Memory of Her*. New York: Crossroad Publishing Company.

---. 1984. *Bread Not Stones*. Boston: Beacon Press.

---. 1985. "The Will to Choose or to Reject." In *Feminist Interpretation of the Bible*. *See* Russell 1985.

---. 1992. *But She Said*. Boston: Beacon Press.

---. 1993. *Discipleship of Equals*. New York: Crossroad Publishing Company.

Fischel, Henry. 1969. "Story and History: Observations on Greco-Roman Rhetoric and Pharisaism." In *American Oriental Society, Middle West Branch, Semi Centennial Volume*. Edited by Denis Senior. Bloomington: Indiana University Press.

Fisher, Eugene. 1984. "Research on Christian Teaching Concerning Jews and Judaism: Past Research and Present Needs." *Journal of Ecumenical Studies* 21:421-437.

Flatters, Jutta. 1988a. "Rezension zu C. Mulacks *Jesus der Gesalbte der Frauen*." *Schlangenbrut* 29:48

---. 1988b. "Von der Aufwertung des Weiblichen und ihrem Preis: Kritische Anmerkungen zu *Jesus der Gesalbte der Frauen*." In *Verdrängte Vergangenheit, die uns bedrängt. See* Siegele-Wenschkewitz 1988.

Flusser, David. 1969. *Jesus*. Translated by Ronald Walls. New York: Herder and Herder.

Folz, Hans. [1480] 1908. "Pharetra contra iudeaos: Der Köcher wider die juden." In *Die Meisterlieder des Hans Folz*. Edited by August L. Mayer. Berlin: Weidmann'sche Buchhandlung.

Foucault, Michel. 1972. *The Archeology of Knowledge*. Translated by A.M. Sheridan Smith. New York: Pantheon Books.

---. 1984. *The Foucault Reader*. Edited By Paul Rabinow. New York: Pantheon Books.

Fromm, Erich. [1956] 1974. *The Art of Loving*. San Francisco: Harper & Row Publishers.

Frymer-Kensky, Tikva Simone. 1992. *In the Wake of the Goddesses: Women, Culture, and the Biblical Transformation of Pagan Myth.* New York: The Free Press.

Fuchs, Esther. 1985. "The Literary Characterization of Mothers and Sexual Politics in the Hebrew Bible." In *Feminist Perspectives on Biblical Scholarship. See* A. Y. Collins 1985.

Fuchs-Kreimer, Nancy. 1981. "Christian Old Testament Theology: A Time for New Beginnings." *Journal of Ecumenical Studies* 18:76-92.

Gage, Mathilde. [1893] 1980. *Woman, Church & State.* Watertown, MA: Persephone Press.

Gager, John. 1985. *The Origins of Anti-Semitism: Attitudes Towards Judaism in Pagan and Christian Antiquity.* New York: Oxford University Press.

Gaston, Lloyd. 1979. "Paul and Torah." In *Antisemitism and the Foundation of Christianity. See* Davies 1979.

---.   1986. "Paul and the Law in Galatians 2-3." In *Anti-Judaism In Early Christianity: Paul and the Gospels.* Vol 1.   Edited by Peter Richardson. Waterloo, Ont.: Wilfried Laurier University Press.

Geertz, Clifford. 1973. *The Interpretation of Cultures.* New York: Basic Books.

Gerber, Uwe. 1987. *Die feministische Eroberung.* Munich: Süddeutscher Verlag.

Gerlach, Wolfgang. 1987. *Als die Zeugen schwiegen: Bekennende Kirche und die Juden.* Berlin: Institut Kirche und Judentum.

Gifford, Carolyn De Swarte. 1985. "American Women and the Bible: The Nature of Woman as a Hermeneutical Issue." In *Feminist Perspectives on Biblical Scholarship. See* A. Y. Collins 1985.

Gilkes, Cheryl Townesend. 1989. "'Mother to the Motherless, Father to the Fatherless.' Power, Gender, and Community in Afrocentric Biblical Tradition." In *Semeia: Interpretation for Liberation* 47:57-87. Edited by Cannon and Schüssler Fiorenza. Atlanta: GA: Scholars Press.

Gilligan, Carol. 1982. *In A Different Voice.* Cambridge, MA: Harvard University Press.

---. 1986. "A Different Voice in Moral Decisions." In *Speaking of Faith.* Edited by Diana L. Eck and Devaki Jain. Philadelphia: New Society Publishers.

Gilman, Sanders. 1985. *Difference and Pathology.* Ithaca: Cornell University Press.

Giordano, Ralph. 1987. *Die zweite Schuld, oder von der Last Deutscher zu sein.* Hamburg: Rasch und Rohring.

Glock, Charles. 1966. *Christian Beliefs and Anti-Semitism*. New York: Harper & Row Publishers.

Goldblatt, David. 1975. "The Beruriah Traditions." *Journal of Jewish Studies* 26 (1-2):68-85.

Goldenberg, Naomi. 1979. *Changing of the Gods: Feminism and the End of Traditional Religion*. Boston: Beacon Press.

Goldstein, Judith. 1986. "Antisemitism, Sexism and the Death of the Goddess." In *Antisemitism in the Contemporary World*. Edited by Michael Curtis. Boulder: Westview Press.

Gordon, Linda. 1986. "What's New in Women' History." In *Feminist Studies, Critical Studies*. Edited by Teresa de Lauretis. Bloomington: Indiana University Press.

Gorsuch, Richard L. and Daniel Aleshire. 1974. "Christian Faith and Ethnic Prejudice: A Review and Interpretation of Research." *Journal of the Scientific Study of Religion* 13:281-305.

Gössmann, Elisabeth. 1983. *Die streitbaren Schwestern*. Freiburg: Herder Verlag.

Göttner-Abendroth, Heide. 1980. *Die Göttin und ihr Heros*. Munich: Frauenoffensive.

---. 1982. *Die tanzende Göttin*. Munich: Frauenoffensive.

---. 1983. "Du Gaia bist ich." In *Feminismus, Inspektion der Herrenkultur*. Edited by Luise Pusch. Frankfurt: Suhrkamp.

Grant, Jacquelyn. 1970. "Black Theology and the Black Woman." In *Black Theology*. Edited by Gayraud S. Wilmore and James Cone. Maryknoll, NY: Orbis Books.

---. 1989. *White Womens' Christ and Black Women's Jesus; Feminist Christology and Womanist Response*. Atlanta, GA: Scholars Press.

Graves, Robert [1948] 1978. *The White Goddess*. New York: Octagon Books.

Gray, Elizabeth Dodson. 1994. *Sunday School Manifesto: In the Image of Her?* Wellesly, MA: Roundtable Press.

Green, Arthur. 1983. "Bride, Spouse, Daughter: Images of the Feminine in Classical Jewish Sources." In *On Being a Jewish Feminist. See* Heschel 1983.

Griffin, Susan. 1978. *Woman and Nature*. New York: Harper & Row Publishers.

---. 1981. *Pornography and Silence*. San Francisco: Harper & Row Publishers.

Griscom, Joan L. 1985. "On Healing the Nature/History Split in Feminist Thought." In *Women's Consciousness, Women's Conscience*. Edited by Barbara Hilkert Andolsen, Christine Gudorf and Mary Pellauer. Minneapolis: Seabury Press.

Grosser, Paul E. and Edwin Halperin. 1979. *Anti-Semitism: The Causes and Effects of a Prejudice*. Secausus: Citadel Press.

Grundmann, Walter. 1940. *Jesus der Galiäer*. Veröffentlichungen des Instituts zur Erforschung des jüdischen Einflusses auf das deutsche kirchliche Leben. Leipzig: G. Wigand.

Guist, Roswita. 1981. *Die religionspädagogische Vertretbarkeit der biblischen Vaterfigur*. Frankfurt: Peter D. Lang Verlag.

Hackett, Jo Ann. 1985. "In the Days of Jael." In *Immaculate and Powerful. See* Atkinson 1985.

---. 1989. "Can A Sexist Model Liberate Us?" *Journal of Feminist Studies in Religion* 5 (1):65-76.

Harding, Sandra. 1986. *The Science Question in Feminism*. Ithaca: Cornell University Press.

Harrison, Beverly. 1985. "The Power of Anger in the Work of Love: Christian Ethics for Women and Other Strangers." In *Making the Connections*. Edited by Carol S. Robb. Boston: Beacon Press.

Hasan-Rokem, Galit and Alan Dundes, eds. 1986. *The Wandering Jew*. Bloomington: Indiana University Press.

Heer, Friedrich. 1967. *God's First Love: Christians and Jews Over Two Thousand Years*. New York: Weybright and Talley.

Heiler, Friedrich. 1939. "Der Dienst der Frau in den Religionen der Menschheit." *Eine heilige Kirche: Zeitschrift für Kirchenkunde und Religionswissenschaft* 21:1-48.

---. 1976. *Die Frau in den Religionen der Menschheit*. Berlin: de Gruyter.

Heine, Susanne. 1986. *Frauen der frühen Christenheit*. Göttingen: Vandenhoeck & Ruprecht. Translated by John Bowden, under the title *Women and Early Christianity: A Reappraisal*. Minneapolis: Augsburg Publishing House, 1988.

---. 1987. *Wiederbelebung der Göttinnen?* Göttingen: Vandenhoeck & Ruprecht. Translated by John Bowden, under the title of *Matriarchs, Goddesses, and Images of God: A Critique of Feminist Theology*. Minneapolis: Augsburg, 1988.

Helie-Lucas, Marie-Aimee. 1990. "Women, Nationalism and Religion in the Algerian Liberation Struggle." In *Opening the Gates: A Century of Arab Feminist Writings*. Edited by Margot Badran and Miriam Cooke. London: Virago Press.

Henry, Sandra and Emily Taitz. 1983. *Written Out of History*. Fresh Meadows, NY: Biblio Press.

Heschel, Susannah, ed. 1983. *On Being A Jewish Feminist*. New York: Schocken.

---. 1986. "Current Issues in Jewish Feminist Theology." *Christian Jewish Relation* 19 (2):23-32.

---. 1988. "Jüdisch-feministische Theologie und Antijudaismus in christlich feministischer Theologie." Translated by Jutta Flatters. In *Verdrängte Vergangenheit, die uns bedrängt*. See Siegele-Wenschkewitz 1988.

---. 1993. "Anti-Semites against Antisemitism." *Tikkun* 8 (November/December): 47-53.

Heyward, Carter. 1982. *The Redemption of God*. New York: Harper & Row Publishers.

---. 1984. *Our Passion for Justice*. New York: Pilgrim Press.

---. 1985. "An Unfinished Symphony of Liberation." *Journal of Feminist Studies in Religion* 1 (1):99-119.

---. 1989. *Speaking of Christ*. New York: Pilgrim Press.

Hildegardstochter, Li. 1987. "Thema: Antisemitismus und feministische Theologie." *Schlangenbrut* 17:32-33.

Hommel, Gisela. 1986. "Der Schreckensgott vom Sinai." *Allgemeine Jüdische Wochenzeitung* 41 (December 19/26):21

---. 1987. "Antisemitic Tendencies in Christian Feminist Theology in Germany." In *European Judaism*. London: Leo Baeck College.

Hoyt, Thomas Jr. 1991. "Interpreting Biblical Scholarship for the Black Church." In *Stony the Road we Trod*. See Felder 1991.

Hügel, Ika, Chris Lange, et. al., eds. 1993. *Entfernte Verbindungen*. Berlin: Orlanda Verlag.

Hull, Gloria T., Patricia Bell Scott and Barbara Smith, eds. 1982. *All The Women Are White, All the Blacks Are Male, But Some Of Us Are Brave*. Old Westbury, NY: The Feminist Press.

Idinopulos, Thomas and Ray Bowen Ward. 1977. "Is Christology Inherently Anti-Semitic? A Critical Review of Rosemary Radford Ruether's *Faith and Fratricide.*" *Journal of the American Academy of Religion* 45 (2):197-223.

Irigaray, Luce. 1985. *Speculum of the Other Woman.* Translated by Gillian C. Gill. Ithaca, NY: Cornell University Press.

Isaac, Jules. 1964. *The Teaching of Contempt.* Translated by Helen Heaver. New York: Holt, Rinehart and Winston.

---. [1948] 1971. *Jesus and Israel.* Translated by Sally Gran. Edited by Claire Huchet. New York: Holt, Rineland and Winston.

Isasi-Diaz, Ada Maria and Yolanda Tarango. 1988. *Hispanic Women.* San Francisco: Harper & Row Publishers.

Jacoby, Jessica and Gotlinde Magiriba Lwanga. 1990. "Was `sie' schon immer über Antisemitismus wissen, wollte, aber nie zu denken wagte." *beiträge zur feministischen theorie und praxis.* Cologne: Sozialwissenschaftliche Forschung und Praxis für Frauen Ev.

Jaggar, Alison M. and Paula Rothenberg, eds. 1984. *Feminist Frameworks.* New York: McGraw Hill Book Company.

Jensen, Anne, Evi Krobath, Elisabeth Moltmann-Wendel, et.al. 1988. "Stellungnahme feministischer Theologinnen zum Vorwurf des Antijudaismus." *Schlangenbrut* 21:36.

Jeremias, Joachim. [1923,1938] 1962. *Jerusalem zur Zeit Jesu.* Göttingen: Vandenhoeck & Ruprecht. Translated by F.H. Cavel, under the title *Jerusalem at the Time of Jesus.* Philadelphia: Fortress Press. 1969.

---. 1965. *The Central Message of the New Testament.* New York: Scribner's Sons.

---. 1966. *Abba: Studien zur neutestamentlichen Theologie und Zeitgeschichte.* Göttingen: Vandenhoeck & Ruprecht.

Jewett, Paul. 1975. *Man as Male and Female.* Grand Rapids: Eerdmans Publications.

Jung, Carl Gustav. 1955. *The Answer to Job.* Translated by R.F.C. Hull. London: Toutledge & Kegan.

Kalven, Janet and Mary Buckley. 1984. *Women's Spirit Bonding.* New York: Pilgrim Press.

Kassel, Maria. 1986. *Das Auge im Bauch.* Freiburg: Walter Verlag.

Katz, Esther and Joan Miriam Ringelheim, eds. 1983. *Women Surviving the Holocaust: Conference Proceedings.* New York: Institute for Research in History.

Katz, Jacob. 1961. *Exclusiveness and Tolerance*. Oxford: Oxford University Press.

---. 1980. *From Prejudice to Destruction: Anti-Semitism, 1700-1933*. Cambridge: Harvard University Press.

Kellenbach, Katharina von. 1986a. "Antisemitismus in biblischer Matriarchatsforschung? Rezension zu *Ich verwerfe im Lande die Kriege* von Gerda Weiler." *Berliner Theologische Zeitschrift* 3:144-148.

---. 1986b. "Jewish-Christian Dialogue on Feminism and Religion." *Christian Jewish Relations* 19 (2):33-40.

---. 1987. "Vom Weyb, Jüd und itlichen teuffelen: Feminismus und Antisemitismus." *Schlangenbrut* 17:40-48.

---. 1988. "Plädoyer zur Überwindung von Androzentrismus und christlichem Triumphalismus." In *Verdrängte Vergangenheit, die uns bedrängt. See* Siegele-Wenschkewitz 1988.

Keller, Catherine. 1986a. "Feminist Reflections on Separation and Unity in Jewish Theology." *Journal of Feminist Studies in Religion* 2 (1):118-121.

---. 1986b. *From A Broken Web*. Boston: Beacon Press.

Klein, Charlotte. 1978. *Anti-Judaism in Christian Theolgy*. Translated by Edward Quinn. Philadelphia: Fortress Press.

Klenicki, Leon. 1983. "The Theology of Liberation: A Latin American Jewish Exploration." *American Jewish Archives* 35:27-39.

Klep fisz, Irena. 1982. "Anti-Semitism in the Lesbian/Feminist Movement." In *Nice Jewish Girls. See* E. T. Beck 1982.

Kohn, Johanna. 1986. *HaShoa: Christlich-jüdische Verständigung nach Auschwitz*. Munich: Kaiser Verlag.

Kohn-Roelin, Johanna. 1987. "Christlicher Feminismus nach Auschwitz: Aspekte einer geschichtlichen Selbstvergewisserung." In *Weil wir nicht vergessen wollen. See* Schaumberger 1987.

Koltun, Elisabeth. 1976. *The Jewish Woman*. New York: Schocken Books.

Kraemer, Ross. 1983. "Women in the Religions of the Greco-Roman World." *Religious Studies Review* 9 (2):127-139.

---. 1985a. "Book Review of *In Memory of Her*." *Religious Studies Review* 11 (1):6-9.

---. 1985b. "A New Inscription from Malta and the Question of Women Elders in the Diaspora Jewish Communities." *Harvard Theological Review* 78:431-438.

---. 1985c. "Non-Literary Evidence for Jewish Women in Rome and Egypt." *Helios* 13 (2):85-101.

---. 1985d. "Review of *In Memory of Her*." *Journal of Biblical Literature* 104 (4):722-725.

---. 1988. *Maenads, Martyrs, Matrons, Monastics: A Source Book on Women's Religion in the Greco-Roman World*. Philadelphia: Fortress Press.

---. 1992. *Her Share of the Blessings*. New York: Oxford University Press.

Kramer, Heinrich and James Sprenger. [1484] 1971. *The Malleus Maleficarum*. Translated by Montague Summers. New York: Dover Publications.

Kühn, Jutta. 1987. "Wenn ein Lehrstuhl am Jungfernhäutchen hängt." *Schlangenbrut* 18:45.

Lacocque, Andre. 1968. "The `Old Testament' in the Protestant Tradition." In *Biblical Studies:Meeting Ground of Jews and Christians*. Edited by Helga Croner. New York: Paulist Press.

Langer, Heidemarie, Herta Leistner, Elisabeth Moltmann-Wendel and Annemarie Schönherr, eds. 1984. *Wir Frauen in Ninive*. Stuttgart: Kreuz Verlag.

Langer, Heidemarie, Herta Leister and Elisabeth Moltmann-Wendel, eds. 1986. *Mit Miriam durch's Schilfmeer*. Stuttgart: Kreuz Verlag.

Laurentin, Rene. 1982. "Jesus und die Frauen: Eine verkannte Revolution." In *Frauen in der Männerkirche. See* Brooten 1982a.

Leipoldt, Johannes. 1921. *Jesus und die Frauen: Bilder aus der Sittengeschichte der alten Welt*. Leipzig: Quelle und Meyer.

---. 1933. *Antisemitismus in der antiken Welt*. Leipzig: Verlag Dörfflin und Franke.

---. 1950. "Antisemitismus." In *Reallexikon für Antike und Christentum*. Stutgart: Hiersmann Verlag.

---. 1955. *Die Frau in der antiken Welt und im Urchristentum*. Leipzig: Köhler und Amelang.

---. 1962. *Die Frau in der Antike und im Urchristentum*. Gütersloh: Gütersloher Verlagshaus.

LeRider, Jacques. 1985. *Der Fall Otto Weininger: Wurzeln des Antifeminismus and Antisemitismus*. Translated from the French by Dieter Hornig. Vienna: Loecker Verlag.

Lerner, Elinor. 1985. "American Feminism and the Jewish Question, 1890-1940." In *Ambiguous Encounter: Antisemitism and the American Left.* Edited by David Gerber. Urbana: University of Illinois Press.

Lerner, Gerda. 1986. *The Creation of Patriarchy.* New York, Oxford: Oxford University Press.

---. 1993. *The Creation of Feminist Consciousness: From the Middle Ages to Eighteen-seventy.* Oxford: Oxford University Press.

Lerner, Michael. 1992. *The Socialism of Fools: Anti-Semitism on the Left.* Escondido, CA: Publisher's Group West.

Levinson, N.P. and Martin Stöhr, eds. 1967. *Anti-Judaismus im Neuen Testament: Exegetische und systematische Studien.* Munich: Kaiser Verlag.

Lifton, Robert. 1986. *The Nazi Doctors.* New York: Basic Books.

Lipstadt, Deborah. 1993. *Denying the Holocaust: The Growing Assault on Truth and Memory.* New York: The Free Press.

Loewenstein, Rudolph. 1951. *Christians and Jews: A Psychoanalytic Study.* Translated by Vera Damman. New York: International University Press.

Lorde, Audre. 1983. "An Open Letter to Mary Daly." In *This Bridge Called My Back.* Edited by Cherrie Moraga and Gloria Anzaldua. Watertown, MA: Persephone Press.

---. 1984. *Sister Outsider.* Turmansburg, NY: Crossing Press.

Maccoby, Hyam. 1983. *The Sacred Executioner.* Colchester, Essex: Thames and Hudson.

Maertens, Thierry. 1969. *The Advancing Dignity of Women.* De Pere, Wisconsin: St. Norbert Abbey Press.

Marcus, Jacob R. 1981. *The Jew in the Medieval World.* New York: Atheneum.

Martin, Tony. 1993. *The Jewish Onslaught: Dispatches from the Wellesly Front.* Dover, MA: The Majority Press.

McFague, Sally. 1982. *Metaphorical Theology.* Philadelphia: Fortress Press.

McGarry, Michael. 1982. *Christology after Auschwitz.* New York: Paulist Press.

McNamara, Jo Ann. 1976. "Sexual Equality and the Cult of Virginity in Early Christian Thought." *Feminist Studies* 3 (3-4):145-158.

Meagher, John C. 1979. "As the Twig Was Bent: Antisemitism in Greco-Roman and Earliest Christian Times." In *AntiSemitism and the Foundations of Christianity. See* A. Davies 1979.

Meeks, Wayne. 1974. "The Image of the Androgyne: Some Uses of a Symbol in Earliest Christianity." *History of Religions 13:165-208.*

---. 1986. *The Moral World of the First Christians.* Philadelphia: Westminster Press.

Mercadante, Linda. 1988. "Racism in the Women's Movement." In *Journal of Feminist Studies in Religion* 4 (1):94-98.

Meyers, Carol. 1988. *Discovering Eve.* New York: Oxford University Press.

Mollenkott, Virginia. 1977. *Men, Women and the Bible.* Nashville: Abingdon Press.

---. 1983. *The Divine Feminine.* New York: Crossroad Publishing Company.

---. 1987a. *Godding.* New York: Crossroad Publishing Company.

---, ed. 1987b. *Women of Faith in Dialogue.* New York: Crossroad Publishing Company.

Moltmann, Jürgen. 1981. "The Motherly Father. Is Trinitarian Patripassionism Replacing Theological Patriarchalism?" In *God as Father.* Edited by Johann Baptist Metz and Edward Schillebeeckx. New York: Seabury Press.

Moltmann, Jürgen and Elisabeth Moltmann-Wendel. 1981. "Menschlich werden in einer neuen Gemeinschaft" In *Die Gemeinschaft von Männern und Frauen in der Kirche.* Edited by Constance Parvey. Sheffield: World Council of Churches.

Moltmann-Wendel, Elisabeth, ed. 1974. *Menschenrechte für die Frau.* Munich: Kaiser Verlag.

---. 1977. *Freiheit, Gleichheit, Schwesterlichkeit.* Munich: Kaiser Verlag. Translated by Ruth Gritsch, under the title *Liberty, Equality, Sisterhood: On the Emancipation of Women in Church and Society.* Philadelphia: Fortress Press, 1978.

---. 1978. *Frauenbefreiung.* Munich: Kaiser Verlag.

---. 1980. *Ein eigener Mensch werden.* Gütersloh: Gütersloher Verlagshaus. Translated by John Bowden, under the title *The Women around Jesus.* New York: Crossroad, 1982.

---. 1986. *A Land Flowing with Milk and Honey.* Translated from the German by John Bowden. New York: Crossroad Publishing Company. First published as *Land, wo Milch und Honig fließt.* Gütersloh: Gütersloher Verlagshaus, 1985.

Monheim-Geffert, Marga. 1982. "Der Geschlechterkampf im alten Israel." In *Zweimal Patriarchat. See* Rieger 1982.

Moore, George F. 1921. "Christian Writers on Judaism." *Harvard Theological Review* 14:191-254.

Mosse, George L. 1978. *Toward the Final Solution: A History of European Racism.* New York: Howard Fertig.

Muchemblad, Robert. 1979. "The Witches of the Cambresis." In *Religion and the People.* Edited by James Obelkevich. Chapel Hill: University of North Carolina Press.

Mudflower Collective. 1985. *God's Fierce Whimsy.* New York: Pilgrim Press.

Müller, Franziska. 1982. "Paulus und sein Schreiber." In *Zweimal Patriarchat. See* Rieger 1982.

Mulack, Christa. 1983. *Die Weiblichkeit Gottes.* Stuttgart: Kreuz Verlag.

---. 1985. *Maria: Die geheime Göttin im Christentum.* Stuttgart: Kreuz Verlag.

---. 1987. *Jesus der Gesalbte der Frauen.* Stuttgart: Radius Verlag.

---. 1988. "Antwort auf Jutta Flatters." *Schlangenbrut* 22:40-41.

Nation of Islam, Historical Research Department. 1991. *The Secret Relationship Between Blacks and Jews.* Chicago: Latimer Associates.

Neumann, Erich. [1955] 1963. *The Great Mother.* Translated from the German by Ralph Manheim. New York: Pantheon Books.

Neusner, Jacob. 1971. *The Rabbinic Traditions About the Pharisees Before 70.* 3 Vols. Leiden, Holland: Brill.

---. 1979a. "Thematic and Systematic Description: The Case of Mishnah's Division of Women." In *Method and Meaning in Ancient Judaism.* Edited by Jacob Neusner. Missoula: Scholars Press.

---. 1979b. "The Talmud." In *The Jewish World.* Edited by Elie Kedourie. New York: Harrison House.

---. 1987. *Judaism and Christianity in the Age of Constantine.* Chicago: University of Chicago Press.

---. 1989. "The Amazing Mishnah." *Moment* (Jan):18-23.

Oberman, Heiko A. 1981. *Wurzeln des Antisemitismus.* Berlin: Severin und Siedler. Translated by James I. Porter, under the title *The Roots of Anti-Semitism: In the Age of Renaissance and Reformation.* Philadelphia: Fortress Press, 1984.

Ochs, Carol. 1977. *Behind the Sex of God*. Boston: Beacon Press.

Ochshorn, Judith. 1981. *The Female Experience and the Nature of the Divine*. Bloomington: Indiana University Press.

---. 1985. "Ishtar and Her Cult." In *The Book of the Goddess*. *See* Olson 1985.

Oepke, Georg. 1939. "Der Dienst der Frau in der urchristlichen Gemeinde." *Neue Allgemeine Missionszeitschrift* 16:39-53.

---. 1957. "Gyne." In *Theologisches Wörterbuch zum Neuen Testament*. Vol 1. Edited by Gerhard Kittel. Stuttgart: Kohlhammer. Translated by Geoffrey W. Bromiley under the title "Gyne" in *Theological Dictionary of the New Testament*. Grand Rapids: Eerdmann Publishing Company, 1964.

---. 1985. "Gyne." In *Theological Dictionary of the New Testament: Abridged Version*. Grand Rapids: Eerdman Publishing Company.

O'Faolain, Julia and Lauro Martines, eds. 1973. *Not In God's Image*. San Francisco: Harper & Row Publishers.

Olivier, Antje. 1987. "Hexenjagd auf evangelisch: Der Fall Elga Sorge." *Schlangenbrut* 18:56-48.

Olson, Carl, ed. 1985. *The Book of the Goddess*. New York: Crossroad Publishing Company.

Orlinsky, Harry Meyer. 1960. *Ancient Israel*. Ithaca: Cornell University Press.

Ortner, Sherry. 1974. "Is Female to Male as Nature Is To Culture?" In *Woman, Culture and Society*. Edited by Michelle Zimbalist Rosaldo and Louise Lamphere. Stanford, CA: Stanford University Press.

Osten-Sacken, Peter von der. 1977. "Paulinisches Gesetzesverständnis im Spannungsfeld von Eschatologie und Geschichte." *Evangelische Theologie* 37 (Nov/Dec):549-587.

---. 1982. *Grundzüge einer Theologie im christlich-jüdischen Gespräch*. Munich: Kaiser Verlag.

Otwell, John. 1977. *And Sarah Laughed*. Philadelphia: Westminster Press.

Ozick, Cynthia. 1983. "Notes Towards Finding the Right Question." In *On Being A Jewish Feminist*. *See* Heschel 1983.

Pagels, Elaine. 1979. *Gnostic Gospels*. New York: Random House.

Parkes, William James. 1963. *Antisemitism*. Chicago: Quadrangle Books.

---. 1974. *The Conflict of the Church and the Synagogue*. New York: Hermon Press.

---. [1938] 1976. *The Jew in the Medieval Community*. New York: The Soncino Press.

Parvey, Constance. 1974. "The Theology and Leadership of Women in the New Testament." In *Religion and Sexism. See* Ruether 1974b.

Patai, Ralf. 1967. *The Hebrew Goddess*. New York: Ktav Books.

Pawlikowski, John. 1979. "The Historicizing of the Eschatological: The Spiritualization of the Eschatological: Some Reflections." In *AntiSemitism and the Foundations of Christianity. See* A. Davies 1979.

---. 1982. *Christ in the Light of Christian-Jewish Dialogue*. New York: Paulist Press.

Phillips, John A. 1984. *Eve: The History of an Idea*. San Francisco: Harper & Row Publishers.

Plaskow, Judith. 1982. "Blaming Jews for Inventing Patriarchy." In *Nice Jewish Girls. See* E. T. Beck 1982. First published *Lilith* (1979) 7:9-11, 14-17.

---. 1984. "Anti-Semitism: The Unacknowledged Racism." In *Womanspirit Bonding. See* Kalven 1984.

---. 1990. *Standing Again at Sinai: Judaism from a Feminist Perspective*. San Francisco: Harper & Row, Publishers.

---. 1991. "Feminist Anti-Judaism and the Christian God." *Journal of Feminist Studies* 7 (2):99-109.

Plaskow, Judith and Carol Christ, eds. 1989. *Weaving the Visions*. San Francisco: Harper & Row Publishers.

Pogrebin, Letty Cottin. 1982. "Anti-Semitism in the Women's Movement." *Ms* (June):45-72.

Poliakov, Leon. 1965-1976. *The History of Anti-Semitism*. 3 Vols. Translated from the French by Richard Howard. New York: Vanguard Press, Inc.

Pomeroy, Sarah. 1975. *Goddesses, Whores, Wives, and Slaves*. New York: Schocken Books.

Pope, Juliet. 1986. "Anti-Racism, Anti-Zionism and Antisemitism - Debates in the British Women's Movement." *Patterns of Prejudice* 20 (3):13-27.

Pui-Lan, Kwok. 1988. "Mothers and Daughters, Writers and Fighters." In *Inheriting our Mothers' Garden: Feminist Theology in Third World Perspective. See* Russell 1988.

Raming, Ida. 1982. "Von der Freiheit des Evangeliums zur versteinerten Männerkirche." In *Frauen in der Männerkirche. See* Brooten 1982a.

Reichel, Sabine. 1989. *What Did You Do In The War, Daddy? Growing Up German.* New York: Hill and Wang.

Rendtorff, Rolf. 1980. "Die jüdische Bibel und ihre antijüdische Auslegung." In *Auschwitz, Krise der christlichen Theologie.* Edited by Rolf Rendtorff and Ekkehard Stegemann. Munich: Kaiser Verlag.

---. 1981. "Die Hebräische Bibel als Grundlage christlich-theologischer Aussagen über das Judentum." In *Jüdische Existenz und die Erneuerung der christlichen Theologie.* Edited by Martin Stöhr. Munich: Kaiser Verlag.

Renninger, Monika. 1987. "Eine innere Kraft mit Sanftheit und Mitgefühl verbinden." In *Weil wir nicht vergessen wollen. See* Schaumberger 1987.

Rieger, Renate, ed. 1982. *Zweimal Patriarchat.* Bonn: Arbeitsgemeinschaft katholischer Studenten und Hochschulgemeinden (AGG).

---, ed. 1984. *Schlangenlinien.* Bonn: Arbeitsgemeinschaft katholischer Studenten und Hochschulgemeinden (AGG).

---. 1985. "Half of Heaven Belongs to Women and They Must Win it For Themselves: An Attempt at a Feminist Theological Stock-Taking in the Federal Republic of Germany." *Journal of Feminist Studies in Religion* 1 (1):133-145.

Ringe, Sharon. 1985. "A Gentile Woman's Story." In *Feminist Interpretation of the Bible. See* Russell 1985.

Ringelheim, Joan. 1993. "Women and the Holocaust: A Reconsideration of Research." In *Different Voices:Women and the Holocaust.* See Rittner 1993.

Rittner, Carol and John K.Roth. 1993. *Different Voices: Women and the Holocaust.* New York: Paragon House.

Rivkin, Ellis. 1978. *A Hidden Revolution: The Pharisees Search For The Kingdom Within.* Nashville: Abingdon Press.

---. 1984. *What Crucified Jesus: The Political Crucifixion of a Charismatic.* Nashville: Abingdon Press.

Röhm, Eberhard and Jörg Thierfelder. 1982. *Evangelische Kirche zwischen Kreuz und Hakenkreuz: Bilder und Texte einer Ausstellung.* Stuttgart: Calwer Verlag.

Ruether, Rosemary Radford. 1974a. *Faith and Fratricide.* New York: Seabury Press.

---. 1974b. "Misogyny and Virginal Feminism." In *Religion and Sexism.* Edited by Ruether. New York: Simon and Schuster.

---. 1975. *New Woman New Earth.* New York: Seabury Press.

---. 1977. "Anti-Semitism and Christian Theology." In *Auschwitz: Beginning of A New Era?* Edited by Eva Fleischner. New York: Ktav Books.

---. 1979a. "The *Faith and Fratricide* Discussion: Old Problems and New Dimensions." In *AntiSemitism and the Foundations of Christianity. See* A. Davies 1979.

---. 1979b. "Motherearth and the Megamachine." In *Womanspirit Rising. See* Christ 1979.

---. 1980. "Goddesses and Witches: Liberation and Countercultural Feminism." *The Christian Century* (Sept. 10-17):842-847.

---. 1981. *To Change the World.* New York: Crossroad Publishing Company.

---. 1983. *Sexism and God-Talk.* Boston: Beacon Press.

---. 1985. *Womanguides.* Boston: Beacon Press.

---. 1986. "Feminist Spirituality and Historical Religion: Renewal or New Creation?" *Harvard Divinity Bulletin* 16 (3):5-11.

---. 1987. "Female Symbols, Values, and Contexts." *Christianity and Crisis* 46 (19):460-464.

---. 1989. "Sexism and God Language." In *Weaving the Visions. See* Plaskow 1989.

---. 1992. *Gaia and God: An Ecofeminist Theology of Earth Healing.* San Francisco: Harper Collins Publishers.

Ruether and Eleanor McLaughlin, eds. 1979. *Women of Spirit.* New York: Simon and Schuster.

Ruether and Herman Ruether.. 1989. *The Wrath of Jonah.* San Francisco: Harper Collins Publishers.

Russell, Letty. 1974. *Human Liberation in a Feminist Perspective--A Theology.* Philadelphia: Westminster Press.

---. 1985. "Authority and the Challenge of Feminist Interpretation." In *Feminist Interpretation of the Bible.* Edited by Letty Russell. Philadelphia: Westminster Press.

---. 1987. *Household of Freedom.* Philadelphia: Westminster Press.

---, ed. 1988. *Inheriting Our Mother's Garden: Feminist Theology in Third World Perspective.* Philadelphia: Westminster Press.

Rylaarsdam, J. Coert. 1984. "Judaism: The Christian Problem." *Face to Face* 11 (Spring):4-8.

Safran, William. 1986. "Problems of Perceiving and Reacting to Anti-Semitism: Reflections of a Survivor." In *Antisemitism in the Contemporary World.* Edited by Michael Curtis. Boulder: Westview Press.

Sallen, Herbert A. 1977. *Zum Antisemitismus in der Bundesrepublik: Methoden und Ergebnisse der empirischen Antisemitismusforschung.* Frankfurt: Haag und Herrchen.

Sanders, E.P. 1977. *Paul and Palestinian Judaism.* Philadelphia: Fortress Press.

Sandmel, Samuel. 1978. *Anti-Semitism in The New Testament?* Philadelphia: Fortress Press.

Sartre, Jean-Paul. [1948] 1965. *Anti-Semite and Jew.* Translated by George J. Becker. New York: Schocken Books.

Schaumberger, Christine, ed. 1987. *Weil wir nicht vergessen wollen. . . zu einer Theologie im deutschen Kontext.* Münster: Morgana Verlag.

Schaumberger, Christine and Monika Maassen, eds. 1986. *Handbuch Feministische Theologie.* Münster: Morgana Verlag.

Schottroff, Luise. 1980. "Frauen in der Nachfolge Jesu in neutestamentlicher Zeit." In *Traditionen der Befreiung.* Edited by Willy Schottroff. Munich: Kaiser Verlag.

---. 1987. "`Anführerinnen der Gläubigkeit' oder `einige andächtige Weiber': Frauengruppen als Trägerinnen jüdischer und christlicher Religion im ersten Jahrhundert n. Chr." In *Weil wir nicht vergessen wollen. See* Schaumberger 1987.

Schroer, Silvia. 1984. "Die Göttin kehrt zurück." *Reformatio* 33 (6):443-448.

Schwartz, Howard Eilberg. 1988. "Israel in the Mirror of Nature: Animal Metaphors in the Ritual and Narrative of Ancient Israel." *Ritual Studies* 1:1-30.

---. 1990. *The Savage in Judaism.* Bloomington: Indiana University Press.

Seltzer, Robert. 1980. *Jewish People, Jewish Thought.* New York: Macmillan Press.

Setel, Drora. 1985. "Prophets And Pornography: Female Sexual Imagery in Hosea." In *Feminist Interpretation of the Bible. See* Russell 1985.

Setel, Drora, Catherine Keller, Marcia Falk, Anne Solomon and Rita M. Gross. 1986. "Feminist Reflections on Separation and Unity in Jewish Theology." *Journal of Feminist Studies in Religion* 2 (1):113-131.

Sichrovski, Peter. 1988. *Born Guilty: Children of Nazis.* New York: Basic Books.

Siegele-Wenschkewitz, Leonore, ed. 1988. *Verdrängte Vergangenheit, die uns bedrängt*. Munich: Kaiser Verlag.

---. 1992. "Ist Institutionalisierung ein feministisches Konzept? Ein Bericht aus der Arbeit der Evangelischen Akademie Arnoldshain." In *Querdenken: Beiträge zur feministisch-befreiungstheologischen Diskussion*. Edited by the Frauenforschungsprojekt zur Geschichte der Theologinnen Göttingen. Pfaffenweiler: Centaurus Verlagsgesellschaft.

Sigal, Phillip. 1987. *The Halakha of Nazareth According to the Gospel of Matthew*. Lanham, MD: University Press of America.

Simmel, Ernst, ed. 1946. *Anti-Semitism*. New York: International University Press.

Sloyan, Gerard. 1973. *Jesus on Trial*. Philadelphia: Fortress Press.

Smith, Barbara. 1984. "Between a Rock and a Hard Place: Relationships Between Black Women and Jewish Women." In *Yours in Struggle*. *See* Bulkien 1984.

Sorge, Elga. 1985. *Religion und Frau*. Stuttgart: Kohlhammer Verlag.

Spretnak, Charlene. 1978. *Lost Goddesses of Early Greece*. Berkely, CA: Moon Books.

---, ed. 1982. *The Politics of Women's Spirituality*. New York: Doubleday.

Stagg, Evelyn and Frank Stagg. 1978. *Woman in the World of Jesus*. Philadelphia: Westminster Press.

Stanton, Elisabeth Cady. [1895, 1898] 1985. *The Woman's Bible*. Edinburgh: Polygon Books.

Starhawk. 1979. *The Spiral Dance*. San Francisco: Harper & Row Publishers.

---. 1983. *Dreaming the Dark: Sex, Magic and Politics*. Boston: Beacon Press.

Steinsaltz, Adin. 1976. *The Essential Talmud*. New York: Bantam Books.

Stendahl, Krister. 1976. *Paul Among Jews and Gentiles*. Philadelphia: Fortress Press.

Stone, Merlin. 1978. *When God Was A Woman*. New York: Harcourt Brace Jovanovich.

---. 1979. *Ancient Mirrors of Womanhood*. Boston: Beacon Press.

---. 1982. "The Great Goddess: Who Was She?" In *The Politics of Women's Spirituality*. *See* Spretnak 1982.

Strack, Herman L. und Paul Billerbeck. 1926. *Kommentar zum Neuen Testament aus Talmud und Midrash*. Munich: Beck'sche Verlagsbuchhandlung.

Swidler, Leonard. 1971. "Jesus Was a Feminist." *South East Asia Journal of Theology* 13:102-110. Translated under the title "Jesu Begegnung mit Frauen: Jesus als Feminist." In *Menschenrechte für die Frau*. *See* Moltmann-Wendel 1974.

---. 1972. "Is Sexism a Sign of Decadence in Religion?" In *Working Group on Women and Religion of the American Academy of Religion Proceedings*. Edited by Plaskow Goldenberg. Atlanta, GA: Scholars Press.

---. 1976. *Women in Judaism*. Metuchen, N.J.: Scarecrow.

---. 1979. *Biblical Affirmations of Woman*. Philadelphia: Fortress Press.

---. 1981. "The Jewishness of Jesus: Some Religious Implications for Christians." *Journal of Ecumenical Studies* (Winter) 18:104-114.

---. 1988. *Yeshua: A Model for Moderns*. Kansas: Sheed & Ward.

Tal, Uriel. 1971. *Religious and Anti-Religious Roots of Modern Anti-Semitism*. New York: Leo-Baeck Institute.

---. 1975. *Christians and Jews in Germany: Religion, Politics, and Ideology in the Second Reich*. Ithaca: Cornell University Press.

Tavard, George. 1973. *Woman in Christian Tradition*. Notre Dame, London: University of Notre Dame Press.

Teubal, Savina. 1984. *Sarah the Priestess*. Athens, Ohio: Ohio University Press.

---. 1990. *Hagar, the Egyptian: The Lost Tradition of the Matriarchs*. San Francisco: Harper & Row.

Thoma, Clemens. 1980. *A Christian Theology of Judaism*. Translated by Helga Croner. New York: Paulist Press.

Thistlethwaite, Susan. 1985. "Every two Minutes: Battered Women and Feminist Interpretation." In *Feminist Interpretation of the Bible*. *See* Russell 1985.

---. 1989. *Sex, Race and God*. New York: Crossroad Publishing Company.

Thürmer-Rohr, Christina. 1987. *Vagabundinnen: Feministische Essays*. Berlin: Orlanda Verlag.

---. 1989. "Mittäterschaft der Frau--Analyse zwischen Mitgefühl und Kälte." In *Mittäterschaft und Entdeckungslust*. Edited by Christina Thürmer-Rohr, Carola Wildt, Martina Emme. et.al. Berlin: Orlanda Frauenverlag.

Thyen, Hartmut. 1979. ". . nicht mehr männlich und weiblich: Eine Studie zu Gal 3,28." In *Als Mann und Frau geschaffen: Exegetische Studien zur Rolle der*

Frau. Edited by Frank Crüsemann & Hartwig Thyen. Gelnhausen, Berlin: Burckhardthaus.

Tolbert, Marie Ann, ed. 1979. *The Bible and Feminist Hermeneutics*. Decatur, GA: Scholars Press.

Trachtenberg, Joshua. [1943] 1983. *The Devil and the Jews*. New York: Jewish Publication Society.

Trevor Roper, H.R. 1956. *The European Witch-Craze of the 16th and 17th Century*. San Francisco: Harper & Row Publishers.

Trible, Phyllis. 1973. "Depatriarchalizing in Biblical Interpretation." *Journal of the American Academy of Religion* 41 (1):30-47.

---. 1979. *God And The Rhetoric of Sexuality*. Philadelphia: Fortress Press.

---. 1984. *Texts of Terror*. Philadelphia: Fortress Press.

Umanski, Ellen. 1989. "Creating a Jewish Feminist Theology." In *Weaving the Visions*. *See* Plaskow 1989.

Van Buren, Paul. 1980. *Discerning the Way*. New York: Seabury Press.

---. 1983. *A Christian Theology of the People of Israel*. New York: Seabury Press.

---. 1987. *A Theology of the Christian Jewish Reality*. San Francisco: Harper & Row Publishers.

Vatican. 1977. "Declaration On The Question Of The Admission Of Women To The Ministerial Priesthood." In *Women Priests: A Catholic Commentary On The Vatican Declaration*. Edited by Arlene and Leonard Swidler. New York: Paulist Press.

Vermes, Geza. 1983. *Jesus and the World of Judaism*. Philadelphia: Fortress Press.

Wacker, Marie-Theres. 1987a. "Die Göttin kehrt zurück: Kritische Sichtung neuerer Entwürfe." In *Der Gott der Männer und die Frauen*. Edited by Wacker. Düsseldorf: Patmos Verlag.

---. 1987b. "Frau-Sexus-Macht: Eine feministische Relecture des Hoseabuches." In *Der Gott der Männer und die Frauen*. *See* Wacker 1987a.

---. 1987c. "Das Patriarchat in uns austreiben--Antijudaismus als Testfall." *Schlangenbrut* 18:36-38.

Wacker, Marie-Theres and Bernd Wacker. 1988. "Matriarchale Bibelkritik--ein antijudaistisches Konzept?" In *Verdrängte Vergangenheit*. *See* Siegele-Wenschkewitz 1988.

Waters, John W. 1991. "Who Was Hagar?" In *Stony the Road We Trod. See* Felder 1991.

Weems, Renita. 1988. *Just a Sister Away.* San Diego, California: Luramedia.

Wegner, Judith Romney. 1988. *Chattel or Person: The Status of Women in the Mishnah.* New York: Oxford Press.

Wehr, Demaris. 1987. *Jung & Feminism.* Boston: Beacon Press.

Weiler, Gerda. 1984. *Ich verwerfe im Lande die Kriege.* Munich: Frauenoffensive.

---. 1985. *Der enteignete Mythos.* Munich: Frauenoffensive.

---. 1987a. "Gespräch mit Gerda Weiler." *Schlangenbrut* 17:30-31

---. 1987b. "Zur Psychologie des Bösen. Der Versuch einer Verständigung mit K.v. Kellenbach." *Schlangenbrut* 18:32-36.

---. 1989. *Das Matriarchat im Alten Israel.* Stuttgart: Kohlhammer Verlag.

Weininger, Otto. [1903] 1980. *Geschlecht und Charakter: Eine prinzipielle Untersuchung.* Munich: Metthes and Seitz Verlag.

Williams, Delores. 1989. "Womanist Theology." In *Weaving the Visions. See* Plaskow 1989.

---. 1993. *Sisters in the Wilderness: The Challenge of Womanist God-Talk.* Maryknoll, New York: Orbis Press.

Williamson, Clark. 1979. "Christ against the Jews: Review of Sobrino." *Encounter* 40 (Fall):403-412.

---. 1980. "Anti-Judaism in Process Christologies?" *Process Studies* 10 (3-4):73-92.

---. 1982. *Has God Rejected His People?* Nashville: Abingdon Press.

---. 1993. *A Guest in the House of Israel: Post-Holocaust Church Theology.* Louisville, KY: Westminster/John Knox Press.

Wilson-Kastner, Patricia. 1983. *Faith, Feminism and the Christ.* Philadelphia: Fortress Press.

Wolff, Hanna. 1979. *Jesus der Mann.* Stuttgart: Radius Verlag.

---. 1981. *Alter Wein--Neue Schläuche.* Stuttgart: Radius Verlag.

Woolf, Virginia, [1929] 1957. *A Room Of One's Own.* New York: A Harvest/HBJ Book.

INDEX

Aaron, 99
Abba, 75-78
Abraham, 101, 107
Abram, 88
Adam, 23, 107, 124
Adler, Margot, 91
Adultery, 59, 93, 118
African-Americans, 10, 27, 34
African-American women, 87-89. *See also* Black women; Womanist
Agunah, 61
Akiba, 61
Akkedah, 102
Alexandria, 53, 112, 138
Ambiguity, 47
American feminism, 9, 35-36, 97, 139-40
Amoraim, 113
Anat. *See* Goddess, Canaanite
Andolsen, Barbara, 18
Androcentrism, 21, 25, 30, 105
Anger, 1, 2, 14
Anima, 83-86
Antichrist, 24
Antisemitism: definition, 3, 10-13, 39-42; discussion, 4, 9, 33-35, 135-36; effects on Gentiles, 3-7, 9, 10, 136-37; effects on Jews 19-28, 50, 52-53, 139; feminist, 28-36, 110, 116, 121; resistance to Nazi, 7-8, 35, 57; and sexism, 17-27, 31, 129. *See also* Anti-Judaism
Antithesis: conclusion 133; defined, 19, 41-45; of Christianity, 72, 74-75, 78, 86, 88; of Goddess, 91, 101-04, 106; Lutheran, 44, 82
Antithetical, 19, 44, 59, 65-66, 75, 92, 96, 103, 107
Anti-Jewish myth, 24, 28, 40, 42, 50, 133-34, 140

Anti-Judaism: in Christian theology, 37-40; combatting, 134-38; definition of, 10-14; in Germany, 33-36
Anti-Zionism, 12, 52, 99, 110, 135
Aphrodite. *See* Goddess, Greek
Appropriation, 125-27
Aristotle, 78
Aryan, 11, 58, 116. *See also* Non-Aryan
Assyria, 96, 108
Augustine, 20
Auschwitz, 34
Austen, Ralph, 89
Authoritarianism, 75-78, 101-03, 121, 133
Azzai, Rabbi, 68

Baader, Maria, 36
Baal, 98, 114, 117
Babylonia, 93, 108, 115
Babylonian Talmud. *See* Talmud
Bachofen, Johann Jacob, 91-92
Balch, David, 71, 73
Baptism, 11, 65, 130
Baptismal formula, 72
Barr, James, 76
Beck, Evelyn Torton, 31
Beck, Norman, 40
Biale, Rachel, 61, 68
Binford, Sallie, 92
Bitton-Jackson, Livia, 21
Black: church, 76, 86-87; death, 50; theology, 87; women, 17, 22, 36, 127
Blasphemy, 48, 116
Blenkinsopp, Joseph, 44
Blood libel, 50
Boneh, Nahum, 6
Boyarin, Daniel, 67-68, 103
Brandon, Samuel G., 48
Bratton, Fred Glaston, 48
Bridenthal, Renate, 25

Massen, Monika, 32
Maternal love, 81-83, 116
matriarchy: destruction of, 107-13; in
    Hebrew Bible, 8, 95; as religion,
    78-79, 81, 91-111; restored by
    Jesus, 83, 115-18; as social
    system, 91-96. *See also* Goddess;
    Neo-pagan; Polytheism
McCauley, Deborah, 29-30, 102, 125
McFague, Sally, 75, 78-79, 118
McGarry, Michael, 54
McLaughlin, Eleanor, 125
McNamara, Jo Ann, 124
Meeks, Wayne, 70, 72
Menstruation, 59, 68, 111-13
Mercadante, Linda, 76
Mesopotamia, 93, 98
Messiah, 116
Meyers, Carol, 95, 109
Middle Ages, 11, 24, 50
Middle Assyrian Law, 93
Midrash, 72-73, 82
Militarism, 96-101, 120, 133. *See*
    also Violence
Miriam, 99
Mishnah, 61, 67, 113, 124
Mollenkott, Virginia, 29, 58, 60, 127
Moltmann, Jürgen, 78
Moltmann-Wendel, Elisabeth, 33, 58,
    66, 76, 81, 83, 111, 118, 124
Monheim-Geffert, Marga, 92, 107
Monolatry, 80, 105-06
Monotheism: and intolerance, 100,
    113-15, 120-24; and patriarchy
    78-81, 93-94, 105-07. *See also*
    God
Moore, George F., 46
Moral, 20, 82
Moses, 99
Mowinkel, 100
Mudflower Collective, 17
Mulack, Christa, 76, 83-84, 101-02,
    104, 113, 117-18, 121, 126-27
Myth of feminine evil, 23, 107

National Council of Christians and
    Jews, 29
Nation of Islam, 89
National Socialism. *See* Nazi
Nature-culture split, 102-04

Nazis: crimes of, 2, 4-7, 24, 120-21,
    137; ideology of, 11, 100, 116;
    paganism of, 35-36
Neo-pagan, 35, 97, 111, 139. *See*
    also Matriarchal; Pagan
Neumann, Erich, 81, 91
Neusner, Jacob, 82
New covenant, 40, 44, 51. *See also*
    Covenant; New covenant
New Testament, 39, 44, 45, 58, 63,
    65, 69, 72, 76-77, 111, 119-20
Niddah. See Menstruation
Non-Aryan, 4, 11-12. *See also* Aryan
Noth, Martin, 51, 123

Oberman, Heiko, 52
Ochs, Carol, 91, 101-04, 117
Ochshorn, Judith, 85, 91, 104, 109
Oepke, Georg, 57-58, 69, 112
O'Faolain, Julia, 23
Old covenant, 40-41, 44, 51-52,
    123-24. *See also* Covenant; Old
    covenant
Old Testament, 8, 41, 51, 77, 116,
    123-24
Oppression: interstructuring of,
    17-19, 28, 31, 129; of Jews, 14,
    127, 138; as problem of oppressor,
    3-4; of women, 15-16, 59
Oriental, 22, 70
Origin of patriarchy: in Christianity,
    111-13; of evil, 24, 120-24; in
    Near East, 106-11, 120-22
Orlinsky, Harry Meyer, 110
Ortner, Sherry, 103
Other, 19, 25, 30-31, 43, 47, 70, 85,
    133
Ozick, Cynthia, 59

Pagan: religion, 78, 97-111, 114-17;
    society, 91-96, 108-10. *See also*
    Goddess; Matriarchy; Neo-Pagan
Pagels, Elaine, 57, 111
Palestine, 69, 107
Palestinian Talmud. *See* Talmud
Paradise, 92, 101, 107, 116
Parkes, William James, 12
Particularism, 42-43
Particularity, 85-86, 129-30. *See also*
    Chosenness; Covenant; Election
Particularization, 135